The Recovery of
Paul's Letter to the Galatians

By the Same Author
The Theology of Acts (S.P.C.K.)
The Puzzle of 1 John (S.P.C.K.)

Stud

The Recovery of
Paul's Letter to the Galatians

J. C. O'NEILL

LONDON

S·P·C·K

1972

First published in 1972
by S.P.C.K.
Holy Trinity Church
Marylebone Road
London NW 1 4DU

Printed in Great Britain by
William Clowes & Sons, Limited
London, Beccles and Colchester

TO

J. Y. C.

SBN 281 02678 5

CONTENTS

v

NOTES ON
PASSAGES

PREFACE

I should like to thank the students of Westminster College, with whom I read Galatians in Lent Term, 1967, for helping me to think hard about the epistle; the Alexander von Humboldt Stiftung for giving me a grant to work for three months in Göttingen; and my colleagues at Westminster, and the College Committee of the Presbyterian Church of England, who made it possible for me to take up this opportunity to go to Germany in the summer of 1967.

Westminster and Cheshunt Colleges, Cambridge   J.C.O'N.

ABBREVIATIONS

Bauer-A. G.   A Greek–English Lexicon of the New Testament and Other Early Christian Literature. A translation and adaptation of Walter Bauer's *Griechisch-Deutsches Wörterbuch* . . . by William F. Arndt and F. Wilbur Gingrich. Cambridge and Chicago 1957

ET   *The Expository Times*

JTS   *The Journal of Theological Studies*

NTS   *New Testament Studies*

ThLZ   *Theologische Literaturzeitung*

TU   *Texte und Untersuchungen zur Geschichte der altchristlichen Literatur*

ZNW   *Zeitschrift für die neutestamentliche Wissenschaft*

INTRODUCTION

A History of the Interpretation
of Paul's Epistle to the Galatians
in Modern Times
with Reasons for Reviving
an Old Approach

The modern approach to studying the books of the Bible goes back to the seventeenth century, to the first practitioner, Hugo Grotius (1583–1645), and to the first theoreticians, Baruch de Spinoza (1632–77) and John Locke (1632–1704). Spinoza, in chapter VII of *A Theologico-Political Treatise* (1670), laid down the principle of the interpretation of Scripture upon which the modern approach is based. "The universal rule, then, in interpreting Scripture is to accept nothing as an authoritative Scriptural statement which we do not perceive very clearly when we examine it in the light of its history."[1] The "history" of a scriptural statement comprised (i) the nature of the language in which it was written, (ii) an analysis of the book and its arrangement, and (iii) an account of the environment of the book: the author, the occasion, and the reception of the book.

John Locke prefaced his *Paraphrase and Notes on the Epistles of St Paul to the Galatians, I & II Corinthians, Romans, and Ephesians* with "An Essay for the Understanding of St Paul's Epistles, by Consulting St Paul Himself" in which he was politely contemptuous of the theologians' commentaries on Paul.[2] Locke argued that Paul must have been "a coherent, argumentative, pertinent Writer; and Care, I think, should be taken, in expounding of him, to show that he is so".[3]

> The Light of the Gospel he had received from the Fountain and Father of Light himself, who, I concluded, had not furnished him in this extraordinary Manner, if all this plentiful Stock of Learning and Illumination had been in danger to have been lost, or proved useless, in a jumbled and confused Head; nor have laid up such a Store of admirable and useful Knowledge in

I

a Man, who, for want of Method and Order, Clearness of Conception, or Pertinency in Discourse, could not draw it out into
Use with the greatest Advantages of Force and Coherence.[4]

Locke's method was to read the epistles through from beginning
to end a great number of times in order to see the coherence of the
argument. He did not claim to clear up every obscurity, but this,
he thought, was inevitable, since we did not understand all the
allusions, which would have been perfectly plain to the first
readers.

Spinoza and Locke forced us to try to picture the biblical writers
as men with a history writing at a distinct time and place to other
men. The biblical writers must have had a clear message, and
they must have known how to convey that message. Since Spinoza
and Locke, scholars have seen their work as an attempt to con-
struct a picture of how the biblical documents came to be written.
This historical task is now almost universally recognized as the
central work of Christian biblical scholars, a work that is, tan-
talizingly, both independent of the belief of the scholar or his
Church, and all important for that belief.[5]

Once the force of Locke's argument about Paul's coherence is
acknowledged, difficulties begin to arise in reconciling one part of
the Pauline corpus with another, and the Pauline corpus with
Acts. Locke had himself argued from the "force, order and per-
spicuity" of Paul's discourses in Acts to the necessary coherence
of his epistles, but the time would inevitably come when it would
be suggested that Paul was properly represented here and dis-
torted there. The first writer in modern times to deny the authenticity of any of Paul's epistles (leaving Hebrews out of account)
was probably Edward Evanson in a section of thirty pages at the
end of his book, *The Dissonance of the Four Generally Received Evan-
gelists, and the Evidence of Their Respective Authenticity Examined*
(Ipswich 1792). For the Gospels, he had preferred the Histories
of Luke and made them the standard by which to reject Matthew,
Mark, and John, as written in the second century. For the Epistles,
he rejected as authentic Romans, Ephesians, Colossians, Hebrews,
James, 1 and 2 Peter, 1, 2, and 3 John, Jude, and the letters in
Revelation on the ground that they lacked "that necessary in-
ternal testimony of the divine authority of the writer, the spirit of
prophecy", but he accepted 1 and 2 Corinthians, 1 and 2 Thessalonians, Galatians, and 1 and 2 Timothy.[6]

But the debate about the authenticity of Paul's epistles properly began at the beginning of the nineteenth century, when J. E. C. Schmidt, Schleiermacher, and Eichhorn began to reject the Pastoral Epistles. Ferdinand Christian Baur took the discussion to a decisive conclusion by casting doubt on the reliability of the Acts of the Apostles as an account of the history of the early Church, and by distinguishing between three classes of Pauline writings: the inauthentic Pastoral Epistles; the Antilegomena (1 and 2 Thessalonians, Ephesians, Colossians, Philemon, and Philippians), whose genuineness has been and may be called into question; and the Homologoumena (Galatians, 1 and 2 Corinthians, and Romans), the chief epistles, against which not the least suspicion of inauthenticity is or can be raised.[7]

Most New Testament scholars now accept this threefold division (although most would put more epistles into the Homologoumena class) and prefer the epistles to Acts, if they have to choose.

Yet, almost as soon as F. C. Baur had established his position, his conclusions were attacked in a brilliant exegetical book by Bruno Bauer, *Kritik der paulinischen Briefe*, the first part of which, *Der Ursprung des Galaterbriefs* (Berlin 1850), will have to be noticed on almost every page of this book. Bruno Bauer (1809–82)[8] began to write as a Hegelian of the right wing, to defend the miracles in the life of Jesus and his character as incarnation of divine truth against the attacks of David Friedrich Strauss. A book on the Fourth Gospel (1840) in which he argued that this Gospel was a piece of reflective writing, meant to be history, but really importing the ideas of a later age into the account of Jesus, was quickly followed by his *Kritik der evangelischen Geschichte der Synoptiker* (Leipzig 1841–42), which is the forerunner of form-criticism. He had accepted Chr. H. Weisse's conclusion (*Die evangelische Geschichte kritisch und philosophisch bearbeitet*, Leipzig 1838) that Mark was used by Matthew and Luke, but went on from there to argue that Mark, like John, was also the product of the Church's imagination. As he wrote the three volumes, he gave up his former belief that Jesus was the historical person behind the Gospels.

In 1850 Bauer published his work on Acts, in which he announced that he would not be bound by F. C. Baur's alternative, the Acts or the Four Chief Pauline Epistles; could not both presentations be works of free reflection? He concluded that Acts was the expression of the triumph of "Judaism" over the revolutionary movement of "Paulinism".

3

His aim in examining the Pauline epistles was to discover which of them were written before Acts and which after, and what was their relationship to one another. He began with Galatians, and by means of consecutive exegesis argued that the epistle could not have been written by Paul to the congregations to which it purported to be addressed, and that all the ideas and most of the expressions were clumsily derived from Romans and the Corinthian correspondence—indeed, could often only be understood if one knew the original setting. The author of Galatians was, in short, a compiler.

Apart from a brief introduction, the whole part devoted to Galatians—seventy-four pages—is packed with precise, well-argued exegetical observations. The only general weakness in his argument is that no compiler would have made such a bad job of compilation as this author seems to have done; a compiler is more likely to have produced a smooth and understandable epistle than this. The more Bauer vents his sarcasm on the compiler for clumsiness in using his sources, the less likely does he make the hypothesis that a compiler was at work.

Bruno Bauer's book was almost completely ignored for many years.

In 1882, 1883, and 1886 Abraham Dirk Loman (1823–97), a Dutch Lutheran professor, discussed "Quaestiones Paulinae" in the *Theologisch Tijdschrift*, and came to conclusions similar to those of Bruno Bauer. He argued that the historical Paul was friendly to the Jewish Christians, and only the canonical Paul was made their deadly enemy. The historical Paul was close to the Paul we meet in the "we" sections of Acts.

About the same time Allard Pierson and S. A. Naber published *Verisimilia. Laceram conditionem Novi Testamenti exemplis illustrarunt et ab origine repetierunt* (Amsterdam 1886) in which they argued that the New Testament consisted of liberal Jewish writings which later Christians had taken over and adapted. The Pauline epistles were adapted by a "Paulus Episkopus".

But the most solid and balanced revival of Bruno Bauer's hypothesis was by the Swiss Reformed New Testament scholar, Rudolf Steck (1842–1924).[9] The tone of his book, *Der Galaterbrief nach seiner Echtheit untersucht nebst kritischen Bermerkungen zu den paulinischen Hauptbriefen* (Berlin 1888) is summed up in a quotation from Dionysius of Alexandria which he prints at the beginning. Dionysius concluded his discussion of the differences between the

4

Fourth Gospel and the Apocalypse, "For I have not said these things in mockery (let no one think it), but merely to establish the dissimilarity of these writings" (Eusebius, *H.E.* vii. 25.27, tr. J. E. L. Oulton). Steck's conclusions are mostly based on Bauer, except that he gives more credence to the development of events as given in Acts than Bauer had done, although Acts is still seen as tendentious. "If Acts is the work of a conciliatory Paulinist, what we hear in Galatians is the answer of a radical disciple of Paul."[10]

Steck won a few supporters, first Völter[11] and then van Manen,[12] but by the end of the century Bruno Bauer's work seemed to be dead, finished perhaps by Carl Clemen's *Die Einheitlichkeit der paulinischen Briefe* (Göttingen 1894), but finally caught up, together with the vast torrent of writing on Paul that Ferdinand Christian Baur had helped to begin, into the masterly synthesis of Albert Schweitzer. His chapter v, "Critical Questions and Hypotheses" in *Geschichte der paulinischen Forschung von der Reformation bis auf die Gegenwart* (Tübingen 1911; English translation London 1912) is still the best discussion of this important episode in Pauline studies.

Just as Bruno Bauer made a decisive move against Ferdinand Christian Baur only a few years after the definitive statement of the impregnable authenticity of the four chief Pauline epistles (a thesis F. C. Baur was working on from before 1831, and published in book form in 1845), so Christian Hermann Weisse (1801–1866) made a decisive move against Bruno Bauer only a few years after Bauer's book was published. Weisse's criticism is buried in the first volume of his vast *Philosophische Dogmatik oder Philosophie des Christenthums* (Leipzig 1855–62). Weisse has already been mentioned as the man who first propounded the now generally accepted two-document hypothesis to solve the Synoptic Problem, and in 1856 he first put forward the suggestion, which has also found much support, that the Prologue to the Fourth Gospel, together with parts of chapters 3 and 5, contains a source. He was not a New Testament scholar by profession, but a philosopher, who began as a Hegelian, and ended as an idealist propounding a system that was as close as possible to Christian dogma.

He introduced his discussion on Scripture in the *Philosophische Dogmatik* with the argument that only those writings should be recognized as apostolic that have the witness of the Spirit that they could stem from none other than a "bearer of the Spirit".[13]

5

He then remarks that "a critic who is accustomed to working from this mid-point—a living perception of the true spirit and nature of the apostolic personalities—will never be able to share the doubts that have recently been cast by more than a few scholars on the authenticity of some of the epistles that had always been thought apostolic"—almost certainly a reference to Bruno Bauer. But Weisse tacitly recognizes the force of some of Bauer's objections by going on to say,

> In so far as the critic has the true criterion afforded by this perception, he will reap two advantages. On the one hand, the perception will call him back from the excesses that entangle whoever lacks that sort of spiritual criterion and, on the other hand, he will find himself enriched from this very source with new critical insights.[14]

The "new critical insights" are put forward in a note more than four pages long, printed in smaller type.

Weisse argues that 1 Corinthians is a completely authentic example of Paul's writing.

> We possess [in 1 Corinthians] a document from the hand of the Apostle Paul that bears the stamp throughout of complete integrity and authenticity. This offers us such a clear and inwardly vivid picture of his personal characteristics sharply imprinted in the features of the style, that no composition of any other man (as, for example, some follower of the Apostle) could possibly achieve the same effect in a similarly short space.[15]

Two, possibly three, other epistles are equally pure: 2 Corinthians, 1 Thessalonians, and Philemon, but 2 Corinthians has been compiled from three different letters of Paul. Romans and Philippians are also compilations, but in this case the original letters have been interwoven with a continuous series of interpolations, which in some places almost completely destroy the genuine apostolic character of the style. An interpolator has also been at work on Galatians and Colossians, although in these epistles the apostolic basis itself is quite straightforward, not, as in Romans and Philippians, a pastiche. Weisse believed that the compiler and interpolator of Romans and Philippians was also the interpolator of Galatians and Colossians. Fortunately, the interpolator had the highest regard for the apostle's own words and omitted none of them, except the original introductions to two of the letters used in Romans and Philippians.

Weisse got over the difficulty of explaining how the original letters could have been so treated by suggesting that possibly the process had begun under Paul's eyes, with his permission and at his behest. (Weisse thought that Ephesians, 2 Thessalonians, and 1 Timothy were not apostolic, and that 2 Timothy and Titus contained only a tiny apostolic kernel.)

Although Weisse worked hard during his lifetime to establish the true apostolic text of the epistles, his results were not published until after his death, when they were edited by a pupil.[16]

This approach was taken up twenty years later by a number of Dutch scholars, notably van Manen, who argued at first that Marcion's text was the original of Paul, although later he came to believe that the whole epistle was inauthentic,[17] and Jakob Cramer (1833–95). Cramer was Professor of Church History, History of Dogma, and Early Christian Literature, at Utrecht. He was an orthodox theologian who combated modernism and empiricism in the name of biblical supernaturalism, but at the same time he tried to get the Church to see the necessity of taking account of critical scholarship. To this end he co-operated with G. H. Lamers to produce a series of new studies in theology. He wrote short pamphlets on the Gospels, the Epistle to the Philippians, Calvin's attitude to Scripture, Roman Catholic and Protestant attitudes to Scripture, and the doctrine of inspiration. The sixth of these studies was a commentary of 320 pages on Galatians, *De brief van Paulus aan de Galatiërs in zijn oorspronkelijken vorm hersteld, en verklaard* (Utrecht 1890). Unfortunately, I do not read enough Dutch to have been able to follow his arguments, but he prints a reconstructed text at the end, and I have often noted his excisions. R. A. Lipsius in his commentary gives a full account of all the suggested omissions of Weisse, van Manen, Harting, van de Sande-Bakhuyzen, Baljon, Naber, Völter, and Cramer, although he does not think this approach makes any real contribution to understanding Galatians.

Since Cramer, very few New Testament scholars have taken much account of the possibility that Galatians has been glossed or interpolated.[18]

I hope to show in a detailed discussion of the Epistle to the Galatians that Paul's original letter has been both glossed and interpolated, though rarely altered. This I believe to be the most

7

likely solution to the dilemma which inevitably arises once the demand of Spinoza and Locke for a plain reading of the text, the demand that provided the impulse for all modern study of the New Testament, has been faced. The dilemma is that if Paul was "a coherent, argumentative, pertinent writer" (Locke), Galatians as it now stands cannot have been written by Paul, for, as Bruno Bauer demonstrated, Galatians is full of obscurities, contradictions, improbable remarks, and *non sequiturs*; but, if Galatians was not written by Paul, it is too obscure and disjointed, and at the same time too urgent and vital and compelling, to have been written by a compiler. Christian Hermann Weisse saw the way out of the dilemma. Nobody but Paul could have written Galatians, yet the Galatians we possess is not entirely Paul's.

This dilemma can hardly be avoided by supposing that there are plenty of eminent commentators who have made satisfactory and coherent sense of the text in its present form, because these commentators, with access to each other's work, have time and time again had to confess that they do not agree. If *they* cannot agree, it seems to me forbidden to our generation, probably rather less well equipped with philological and general historical knowledge of the early Church and the classical world, to rest in the assumption that the text as we have it is, in principle, capable of yielding coherent sense. Unless we can find another way to make sense of Galatians, we had better give up the struggle, for we are unlikely to follow the old way better than, say, J. B. Lightfoot (1865; 2nd edn, 1866; 10th edn, 1890), R. A. Lipsius (1891; 2nd edn, 1892), Th. Zahn (1905; 2nd edn, 1907; 3rd edn, 1922), H. Lietzmann (1910; 2nd edn, 1923; 3rd edn, 1932), M.-J. Lagrange (1918; 3rd edn, 1926; 4th edn, 1942), A. Oepke (1937; 2nd edn, 1957), and H. Schlier (1949; 2nd edn, 1951; 3rd edn, 1962). One need only observe how their editions overlap, and then compare their notes on such famous *cruces* as the circumcision of Titus (2.3), Paul's attack on Cephas (2.14ff), and the question "Is Christ the minister of sin?" (2.17), or compare their assessment of Paul's attitude to the Law, to see that something is wrong. No doubt each commentator who works on the present text as printed by Nestle or Kilpatrick or Aland comes to terms with the difficulties, and satisfies himself that he has been faithful to Paul's mind, but the fact that a century of such patient and devoted scholarship has yielded so few agreements on difficult passages and fundamental issues makes me think that the nineteenth-century debate is not yet over. However wild and unbalanced were some of the scholars whose work I have been discussing, they were brilliant and well-informed men whose dissatisfaction with the text of Galatians as we now have it was not a figment of their imagination.

The great difficulty about accepting all Galatians as written by Paul is that Paul can scarcely have adopted the attitude towards Judaism that sometimes appears in Galatians. Consider Bruno Bauer's comment on Gal. 1.13, ἠκούσατε γὰρ τὴν ἐμὴν ἀναστροφήν ποτε ἐν τῷ 'Ιουδαϊσμῷ. He asks, When can the faith of Israel have been called Judaism? "First then, when the war against the Law was decided and Judaism had become the category of the obsolete and the pure antithesis to Christianity."[19] Or his comment on στοιχεῖα in 4.3,9 (a passage which, perhaps wrongly, he takes as addressed to Jews). "How long it must have been since Judaism had finally fallen, if its nature could be assigned to the elemental principals of the world, that is, put on the same level as heathenism because of its dependence on natural forces!"[20] The Rabbi M. Joël and Daniel Völter also fastened on this point, a point which is closely bound up with the obscure matter of the exact relations between Paul and Cephas, and Cephas and James.[21] F. C. Baur had made Paul's universalism and Peter's Jewish particularism the basis of his reconstruction of the history of early Christianity, but he and all who followed him were left with the problem of explaining why Paul was so anxious to get the Jerusalem leaders to acknowledge his preaching, and what was the substance of the agreement between them. There are many ways proposed for escaping this dilemma, ways which try to distinguish Peter's position from James's, and both from that of the "Judaizers", and the Judaizers' position from that of the libertines, who would want Paul to sever all connection with Jerusalem. But none of the theories is entirely clear, and most run beyond the available evidence. All leave the central situation obscure. How are we to explain that Paul was an independent apostle, who yet thought he should have his preaching approved in Jerusalem; that the Jerusalem leaders, James, Cephas, and John, solemnly agreed to approve his special work, and yet Cephas was able to act in such a way that Paul had to call him to book publicly at Antioch? The obscurity of the situation as it is presented in Galatians has given a foothold to those who wish to deny completely the authenticity of the book, but it remains an obscurity that is as good a guarantee as any of authenticity, for what falsifier would be so implausible and obscure?

I shall suggest that some of the difficulties have arisen because glossators tried to explain difficulties and fill in details. But, however much the picture has been retouched and repainted, the strong master-strokes have not been completely obscured, and on these we must fix our eyes. They may not fit our preconceptions, but nor do they fit the conceptions of the second-century Church. I think that the clue to the strange relations between Paul and the Jerusalem leaders has been given by the Danish New Testament scholar, Johannes Munck (1904–65).[22] He argued that the Jerusalem leaders and Paul agreed that the conversion of the Gentiles, as well as the conversion of the Jews, was part of God's plan for the world; they differed about strategy, the Jerusalem leaders holding that the Gentiles would come in when Israel had responded, and Paul holding that the conversion of the Gentiles might well have to precede that of the Jews. Munck's exegesis of Galatians I do not find satisfactory, but his insistence that Paul and the Jerusalem leaders could agree that there were two different and distinct missions to be carried out alongside one another provides the key to the relationships at the centre of the epistle. Perhaps this suggestion is also the key to Paul's attitude to Israel and the Law; he may have held that Gentile Christians were bound not to adopt the Law, while still agreeing that Jewish Christians were free to keep the Law. Certainly, once the possibility of a twofold mission is acknowledged, with two sorts of Christian congregations, we must admit the possibility that Paul did not advocate one timeless theology that all Christians were bound to hold without variation. He did have a central principle, justification by faith, which he found in Scripture (our Old Testament), but he possibly admitted two different settings in which justified men could live according to their circumstances and history.

I am feeling my way, and cannot be dogmatic about Paul's theology. I have tried to face every difficulty in Galatians as squarely as possible, and to argue from the text alone in the first place, but I have needed some general picture of the crucial relationship between Paul and the Jerusalem leaders in order to see whether or not Galatians is really in touch with history, and to test whether this remark or that could have been made by Paul. In a sense the argument is circular, because one construction of events is used to exclude remarks that would threaten the construction, but the process is never so simple as that, and can be defended against the charge of circularity. The construction must first stand up to the test that it explains the chief stubborn features of the story, which other constructions leave less well explained. Then every tiny feature of the text must be fitted around the construction, and if more than one author is supposed to have been at work, there must be general textual evidence pointing in that direction, and there must be good reason why the original text would have been added to in the way suggested. Any obscurity in the story of the text is a potential threat to the whole picture. That is why these introductory general remarks can be no substitute for a detailed examination of every verse of the epistle. The only test of my thesis, or of any other thesis, is to work through Galatians line by line, and to see which thesis makes the best sense of the words.

I cannot hope to have been completely right at every point in assigning this verse to Paul, and that to a glossator, and the other to an interpolator; even if the division be right, I can easily have ascribed to Paul what was written by a commentator on Paul, and to a commentator what was written by Paul himself—and one such mistake could affect the whole enterprise. I do not even have the comfort of the support of Weisse and Cramer, except in a few places.

Perhaps the first biblical scholar to have embarked on the task was not Weisse, but the heretic Marcion, and although his results do not seem to be the right ones, the fact that he attempted to discover what Paul originally wrote may be quoted as early evidence that the attempt is necessary. Marcion may not simply have wanted to show that Paul's thought was a little different from the representation of it in the generally accepted epistles; he may have actually heard that Paul's original letters had been overlaid by commentary, without possessing accurate information about what was original and what secondary.

If this approach is right, we end up with the paradoxical result that the distinctively modern attempt to recover Paul's clear historical argument has shown that the older ecclesiastical commentaries, which took every phrase with the utmost seriousness as a source of revelation, were not so absurd in their method of dealing with Galatians after all. It is often almost impossible to recover a clear train of argument from a paragraph, the reason being that it is made up of, perhaps, one pregnant sentence from Paul, a meditation on that sentence by a theologian who wished to apply an argument directed to the Galatian situation of the 50s to the life of all Christians fifty years later, plus a gloss on one word by a scribe interested in clearing up an exegetical puzzle. No wonder modern commentaries are full of long despairing notes in small type in which half-a-dozen solutions are canvassed with little hope of deciding which one is right. At least the older commentaries related each phrase not so much to the context (although the context was never ignored) as to the whole corpus of Christian theology. The contradictory ideas about the Law, for instance, were not left contradictory, but related to a subtle and comprehensive system which, since it arose out of the living history of the Church, could better comprehend the points of view of Paul and his annotators and glossators than a modern system that tried to isolate Paul from other New Testament writers and the later Church, in obedience to Spinoza and Locke's injunctions.

We cannot return simply to the older approach; we are bound to accept Spinoza and Locke for, whether we like it or not, we are heirs of the whole modern awareness of history. We must, at all costs, discover what Paul himself wrote, and we must discover, as precisely as we can, the history of the text of his epistles, from the time they were received by those he first addressed until the time when they were gathered together, in a more or less fixed form, into the Christian canon.

If I am right, and if that history was a history of continual expansion as explanatory and expository notes were added to the text, we may now understand more clearly that the incorporation of Paul's epistles into the canon at all was no arbitrary whim of the second-century Church. If I am right, Paul's epistles were regarded as in some sense regulative, authoritative, yes, canonical, from a very early date. Only such writings are reflected upon, preached from, interpolated, and glossed. Only law codes and revered writings suffer that sort of treatment. The original interpolators and glossators probably did not intend their reflections to be incorporated into the text, but the Church, like the ancient lawyers, probably thought it wise to adopt the dictum, "Always take account of the gloss with the text", and the scribes, in any case, would be careful to omit nothing, as they copied the sacred words.

Christian theology today is confused about the type of authority that should be given to Scripture, if any. This book should make it easier to accord to Paul the authority due to him, and also make it easier to accord to the later theologians the lesser authority due to them for their insights into the doctrinal consequences of the apostle's teaching. No historical study of an ancient document can decide the question of its authority, but unless Christians in each generation are convinced again that the documents upon which the Church bases her preaching, worship, and teaching are inspired, they will cease to pay attention. I hope than an historical study that removes obscurities and explains the meaning of the words will help to clear the way for a fresh conviction that Paul was in fact an apostle of the Son of God.

NOTES

1. Regula igitur universalis interpretandi Scripturam est, nihil Scripturae tanquam eius documentum tribuere, quod ex ipsius historia quam maxime perspectum non habeamus. The translation is by R. H. M. Elwes, *The Chief Works of Benedict de Spinoza*, vol. i (1883), p. 101.
2. 4th edn (1742).
3. Ibid., p. xiv.
4. Ibid., p. xiii.
5. Spinoza's dictum, "We are at work not on the truth of passages, but solely on their meaning", opened up a false dichotomy between truth and meaning, although it was valuable at the time in allowing the historical method freedom to develop.
6. Op. cit., pp. 255–85; quotation from p. 284. There was a 2nd edn (Gloucester 1805).
7. *Paulus, der Apostel Jesu Christi &c.* (1st edn, Stuttgart 1845; 2nd posthumous edn, 1867; English translation 1875–6), Second Part, Introduction.
8. See Martin Kegel, *Bruno Bauer und seine Theorien über die Entstehung des Christentums* (Leipzig 1908).
9. About the same time Johannes Friedrich (1836–1917), an Old Catholic professor in Munich, who had been excommunicated from the Roman Catholic Church in 1872 for his opposition to the Vatican Council I, came to the same conclusions independently. He published them in a book which was also an attempt to promote a simplified German spelling, *Die unechtheit des galaterbrifes. Ein beitrag zu einer kritischen geschichte des urchristentums* (Halle 1891). He concluded with a discussion of Steck's book, which had appeared after his own was written.
10. Op. cit., p. 120.
11. Daniel Völter (1855–?), a German Lutheran who in 1885 became professor in the State University of Amsterdam and at the same time professor in the Lutheran seminary, announced his conversion in an article, "Ein Votum zur Frage nach der Echtheit, Integrität und Composition der Vier Paulinischen Hauptbriefe", *Theologisch Tijdschrift* 23 (1889), pp. 265–325. Völter said he was not convinced when he first read Loman, Pierson, and Steck, but came to question the usual views as he worked at Romans in an attempt to settle his own mind. He concluded that Romans and 1 and 2 Corinthians contained a genuine core written by Paul, which had been interpolated. Paul himself could not have rejected the Law in principle, and this point of view has been interpolated from a later time, when

Paul's relative and partial freeing of Gentile Christians from the Law has been overtrumped by the thesis that the Law was entirely superseded. Consequently Völter concluded that Galatians, which was entirely anti-Jewish and antinomian, did not contain even a kernel of Paul's writing. He also held that the pseudonymous letter had been glossed at certain points. He worked out his views in an uncompleted series, of which the first was entitled *Die Komposition der paulinischen Hauptbriefe I: Der Römer- und Galaterbrief* (Tübingen 1890).

12. Willem Christiaan van Manen (1842–1905) was a Dutch Reformed minister and professor at Leiden. At first he opposed Loman and Pierson, but in 1886–87, hesitatingly, and in 1888, decidedly, came out against the authenticity of the four chief epistles. He published a book *Paulus* in three parts: *I De handelingen der Apostelen* (1890), *II De brief aan de Romeinen* (1891), and *III De brieven aan de Korinthiers* (1896). His views had a great influence on English "rationalists", largely because of his articles on "Paul" and "Romans" in *Encyclopaedia Biblica* (1899–1903). Even before his own change of position, he had drawn attention to Bruno Bauer. The anonymous *Antiqua Mater: A Study of Christian Origins* (1887) referred to Bruno Bauer, Loman, van Manen, and the Rabbi M. Joël (*Blicke in die Religionsgeschichte zu Anfang des zweiten christlichen Jahrhunderts* II, 1883); and the author (probably Edwin Johnson) rejected Galatians as inauthentic. The Rt Hon. John Mackinnon Robertson cites van Manen in *Pagan Christs: Studies in comparative hierology* (1903; 2nd edn, 1911), and Thomas Whittaker devoted a book to popularizing van Manen's theories, *The Origins of Christianity with an outline of van Manen's analysis of the Pauline Literature* (1904; 2nd edn, with an appendix on Galatians, 1909; new edn, 1914; 4th edn, with an epilogue, 1933). Whittaker's book encouraged L. Gordon Rylands to produce a much more detailed and scholarly book, *A Critical Analysis of the Four Chief Pauline Epistles: Romans, First and Second Corinthians, and Galatians* (1929). Rylands argued that the kernel of Galatians (approximately 1.1, 2, 6, 9, 11, 12, 15–22; 2.1, 2, 4–16, 18–20; 3.23–8; 4.1–6, 8–20; 5.1) was produced on the basis of the earliest layer in Romans, perhaps by the fourth redactor of Corinthians, not much earlier than A.D. 100. J. M. Robertson in turn influenced P. L. Couchoud, an admirer and friend of Loisy. Couchoud argued that Gal. 1.18–24; 2.6–9; 3.6–9, 15–25; 4.27–30 had been added to Paul's original epistle, and that 3.10–14 and 4.21–6 of the original had been edited; *La Première Édition de St Paul* (Premiers Écrits du Christianisme, Paris 1930).

13. Op. cit., vol. i, p. 143.

14. Ibid., vol. i, pp. 143–4.

15. Ibid., vol. i, p. 145.

16. E. Sulze, *Beiträge zur Kritik der paulinischen Briefe* (Leipzig 1867).

17. "Marcion's brief van Paulus aan de Galatiërs", *Theologisch Tijdschrift* 21 (1887), pp. 382–404; 451–533, and see note 12 above.

18. J. M. S. Baljon, *Exegetisch-kritische verhandeling over den brief van Paulus aan de Galatiërs* (Leiden 1889) recognized a very few glosses in our text of Galatians (notably 1.10 omitting ἢ ζητῶ ἀνθ. ἀρέσκ.; 2.10; 4.25a). D. Völter and L. Gordon Rylands held that an inauthentic Galatians had been glossed and added to (see notes 11 and 12, above). Alfred Loisy, who accepted 1 Thessalonians, Galatians, 1 and 2 Corinthians, Romans, probably Colossians, Philemon, and Philippians as genuine letters of Paul, believed that some of these—1 and 2 Corinthians, 1 Thessalonians, and Romans—were surcharged with interpolations and additions, but held Galatians to be entirely authentic; "Les Épîtres de Paul", *Revue d'Histoire et de Littérature Religieuses* 7 (1921), pp. 76–125; 213–50, at pp. 76–84 and 95–110. P. L. Couchoud thought Galatians had been interpolated (see note 11). A strange theory that the genuine Pauline parts could be distinguished from the later additions by their sound was advocated by Wolfgang Schanze, *Der Galaterbrief* (1st edn, 1918; 2nd edn, 1919) and Eduard Sievers, *Die Paulinischen*

Briefe, Heft 1-3 (1926-29). I have not been able to consult these works. See Gerhard Kittel, "Eduard Sievers' schallanalytische Arbeiten zum N.T.", *ZNW* 30 (1931), pp. 35-49. Ernst Barnikol, in a series of *Forschungen zur Entstehung des Urchristentums, des Neuen Testaments und der Kirche* (Kiel 1929ff), has argued that there are four classes of Pauline epistles: the letters written by Paul (1 and 2 Thessalonians, Galatians, Philemon); the letters or composite letters from the time of conflict that Galatians initiated (1 and 2 Corinthians, Romans, Philippians); the deutero-Pauline letters from after A.D. 70 (Colossians, containing genuine fragments, and Ephesians); and the trito-Pauline letters written after A.D. 100 (the Pastorals). But even the genuine letters have been interpolated, as the titles of two of his studies suggest: *Der nichtpaulinische Ursprung des Parallelismus der Apostel Paulus und Petrus (Galater 2.7-8)* (1931) and *Mensch und Messias: Der nichtpaulinische Ursprung der Präexistenz-Christologie* (1932).

English-speaking scholars have rarely allowed for the possibility that interpolations have been incorporated into our text of Galatians, with the honourable exception of Ernest DeWitt Burton, *A Critical and Exegetical Commentary on the Epistle to the Galatians* (Edinburgh 1921), who regards three verses as possible glosses: 4.25, almost certainly; 3.16b probably; and 3.20. David Warner has argued in a brief article that 2.3-8 is an interpolation, possibly a marginal note by Titus; "Galatians ii.3-8: As an Interpolation", *ET* lxii (September 1951), p. 380.

19. Op. cit., p. 13.
20. Ibid., pp. 50f.
21. Cf. Franz Overbeck, *Uber die Auffassung des Streits des Paulus mit Petrus in Antiochien (Gal. 2.11ff) bei den Kirchenvätern* (Programm zur Rektoratsfeier der Universität, Basel 1877).
22. "Israel and the Gentiles in the New Testament", *JTS* n.s. ii (1951), pp. 3-16; *Paulus und die Heilsgeschichte, Acta Jutlandica XXVI* (Aarhus 1954), English translation, *Paul and the Salvation of Mankind* (1959).

A SELECT LIST OF
MODERN BOOKS AND ARTICLES
ON GALATIANS
in chronological order
arranged according to the date of the author's
first listed contribution to the subject

Baur, Ferdinand Christian, *Paulus, der Apostel Jesu Christi. Sein Leben und Wirken, seine Briefe, und seine Lehre. Ein Beitrag zu einer kritischen Geschichte des Urchristenthums.* 1st edn, Stuttgart 1845; 2nd posthumous edn, ed. E. Zeller, 1867. *Paul: the Apostle of Jesus Christ &c.*, tr. A. Menzies. 2 vols. 1875–6.

Bauer, Bruno, *Kritik der paulinischen Briefe. Erste Abteilung: Der Ursprung des Galaterbriefs.* Berlin 1850.

Hilgenfeld, Adolf, *Der Galaterbrief übersetzt, in seinen geschichtlichen Beziehungen untersucht und erklärt.* Leipzig 1852.

Weisse, Christian Hermann, *Philosophische Dogmatik oder Philosophie des Christenthums.* 3 vols. Leipzig 1855; 1860; 1862.

— *Beiträge zur Kritik der paulinischen Briefe.* A reconstruction of Paul's text, with an introduction by E. Sulze. Leipzig, 1867.

Lightfoot, Joseph Barber, *Saint Paul's Epistle to the Galatians.* 1st edn, 1865; 2nd edn revised, 1866; 10th edn, 1890.

Pierson, Allard, *De Bergrede en andere synoptische fragmenten.* Amsterdam 1878.

Pierson, A., and Naber, S. A., *Verisimilia. Laceram conditionem Novi Testamenti exemplis illustrarunt et ab origine repetierunt.* Amsterdam 1886.

Loman, Abraham Dirk, "Quaestiones Paulinae", *Theologisch Tijdschrift* 16 (1882); 17 (1883); 20 (1886). ("Prolegomena I, II", 16 (1882), pp. 141–85. "Onderzoek naar de echtheid van den brief aan de Galatiërs &c.", 16 (1882), pp. 302–28; 452–87; 17 (1883), pp. 14–51; 52–5; 56–7. "Quaestiones Paulinae II:

Het vraagstuk der echtheid in het licht van de geschiedenis des canons", 20 (1886), pp. 42–113.)

Steck, Rudolf, *Der Galaterbrief nach seiner Echtheit untersucht nebst kritischen Bemerkungen zu den paulinischen Hauptbriefen.* Berlin 1888.

Völter, Daniel, "Ein Votum zur Frage nach der Echtheit, Integrität und Composition der Vier Paulinischen Hauptbriefe", *Theologisch Tijdschrift* 23 (1889), pp. 265–325.

— *Die Komposition der paulinischen Hauptbriefe. I. Der Römer- und Galaterbrief.* Tübingen 1890.

Baljon, Johannes Marinus Simon, *Exegetisch-kritische verhandeling over den brief van Paulus aan de Galatiërs.* Leiden 1889.

Cramer, Jakob, *De brief van Paulus aan de Galatiërs in zijn oorspronkelijken vorm hersteld, en verklaard.* Niewe Bijkragen op het gebied van Godgeleerdheid en Wijsbegeerte, VI. Utrecht 1890.

Lipsius, Richard Adelbert, *Briefe an die Galater, Römer, Philipper.* Hand-Commentar zum Neuen Testament, II.ii. 1st edn, Freiburg i. B. 1891; 2nd edn, cited in this book, 1892.

Clemen, Carl, *Die Einheitlichkeit der paulinischen Briefe an der Hand der bisher mit bezug auf sie aufgestellten Interpolations- und Compilations-hypothesen.* Göttingen 1894.

Zahn, Theodor, *Der Brief des Paulus an die Galater.* Kommentar zum Neuen Testament, IX. 1st edn, Leipzig, 1905; 2nd edn, 1907; 3rd edn, 1922.

Bousset, Wilhelm, *Der Brief an die Galater.* Die Schriften des Neuen Testaments, II. 1st edn, Göttingen 1907; 3rd edn, 1917.

Leitzmann, Hans, *An die Galater.* Handbuch zum Neuen Testament, III, i. 1st edn, Tübingen 1910; 2nd edn, 1923; 3rd edn, 1932.

Schweitzer, Albert, *Geschichte der paulinischen Forschung von der Reformation bis auf die Gegenwart.* Tübingen 1911. *Paul and His Interpreters: A Critical History*, tr. W. Montgomery. 1912.

Loisy, Alfred, *L'Épître aux Galates.* Paris 1916.

— "Les Épîtres de Paul", *Revue d'Histoire et de Littérature Religieuses*, vol. 7 (1921), pp. 76–125, 213–50.

Lagrange, Marie-Joseph, *Saint Paul, Épître aux Galates.* Études Bibliques. Paris 1918; 4th edn, 1942.

Lütgert, Wilhelm, *Gesetz und Geist. Eine Untersuchung zur Vorgeschichte des Galaterbriefes.* Beiträge zur Förderung christlicher Theologie, XXII, 6. Gütersloh 1919.

Burton, Ernest DeWitt, *A Critical and Exegetical Commentary on the Epistle to the Galatians*. The International Critical Commentary. Edinburgh 1921.

Ropes, James Hardy, *The Singular Problem of the Epistle to the Galatians*. Harvard Theological Studies XIV. Cambridge, Mass., 1929.

Duncan, George S., *The Epistle of Paul to the Galatians*. The Moffatt New Testament Commentary. 1934.

Oepke, Albrecht, *Der Brief des Paulus an die Galater*. Theologischer Handkommentar zum Neuen Testament IX. 1st edn, Berlin 1937; 2nd edn, cited in this book, 1957.

Schlier, Heinrich, *Der Brief an die Galater*. Kritisch-Exegetischer Kommentar über das Neue Testament begründet von Heinrich August Wilhelm Meyer VII. 10th edn, Schlier's 1st edn, Göttingen 1949; 2nd edn, 1951; 3rd edn, cited in this book, 1962. (Part or the whole of Schlier's commentary seems to have been published in 1939. It is cited by E. Käsemann, *ZNW* 41 (1942), p. 43, n. 82.)

Munck, Johannes, "Israel and the Gentiles in the New Testament", *The Journal of Theological Studies*, new series, vol. II (1951), pp. 3–16.

— *Paulus und die Heilsgeschichte*. Acta Jutlandica XXVI. Aarhus 1954. *Paul and the Salvation of Mankind*, tr. F. Clarke. 1959.

Bonnard, Pierre, *L'Épître de saint Paul aux Galates*. Commentaire du Nouveau Testament IX. Neuchâtel 1953.

Schmithals, Walter, *Paulus und Jakobus*. Forschungen zur Religion und Literatur des Alten und Neuen Testaments 85. Göttingen 1963. *Paul and James*, tr. D. M. Barton, Studies in Biblical Theology 46. 1965.

NOTES ON PASSAGES

1.1 omit ουδε δι ανθρωπου

The denial that the apostleship was ἀπ' ἀνθρώπων puts Paul in a special category apart from the apostles who had been commissioned by human mediation (2 Cor. 8.23; Phil. 2.25). But it is difficult to understand the force of οὐδὲ δι' ἀνθρώπου. Rhetoric will not explain the change from ἀπό to διά (Lietzmann), because the διά is repeated in the next phrase, διὰ 'Ιησοῦ Χριστοῦ, which would seem 'to give some special unrhetorical distinction to the twice repeated διά in contrast to ἀπό. Such distinction does not exist, however, since the prepositions in the phrases "*from* men" and "*through* Jesus Christ" have exactly the same force. A further difficulty is the change from the plural ἀνθρώπων to the singular ἀνθρώπου. The meaning is not at all obvious. Probably the writer wishes to exclude the suggestion that Barnabas (Acts 11.25f; Zahn) or Ananias (Acts 9.10–19; 22.10–16; Chrysostom) had bestowed the apostleship. But this suggestion has already been excluded by the previous phrase. The difficulty seems more likely to be one that would arise from a reading of Acts by a commentator than that would arise from Paul's own need to guard specifically against a possible misunderstanding. When the words are put aside, the sense is clear and the change of prepositions straightforward (cf. Rom. 3.30; 1 Cor. 12.8; 2 Cor. 3.11).

The gloss was first observed by Cramer.

1.4 omit πονηρου

This verse offers a good example of how a gloss can set off a chain of textual variants. The evidence I wish to discuss is as follows.

(i)   ἐκ τοῦ ἐνεστῶτος αἰῶνος πονηροῦ
      ℵ^c D F G (H) K L P Ψ 69 1908

(ii) ἐκ τοῦ ἐνεστῶτος αἰῶνος τοῦ πονηροῦ
      206 330 635*

19

(iii) ἐκ τοῦ ἐνεστῶτος πονηροῦ αἰῶνος
    489 1873
(iv) ἐκ τοῦ αἰῶνος τοῦ ἐνεστῶτος πονηροῦ
    p⁴⁶ ℵ* A B 33 326
(v) ἐκ τοῦ αἰῶνος τοῦ πονηροῦ
    927 sah
(vi) ἐκ τοῦ ἐνεστῶτος αἰῶνος
    1955 (Lambeth Palace 1186, acc. to Scrivener)

The most awkward text is (i), in which the adjective πονηροῦ sits outside the closed phrase τοῦ ἐνεστῶτος αἰῶνος. Some minuscules show rather clumsy attempts to remedy the text with the minimum of disruption; (ii) provides an article for the hanging adjective, and (iii) brings the adjective into the phrase. The Alexandrian text (iv) is a sophisticated emendation designed to protect what the editors took to be a likely difficult phrase that seemed to be firmly part of the text in the order: τοῦ ἐνεστῶτος πονηροῦ, while remedying the grammar. Many of the versions seem to have simply played down the force of ἐνεστῶτος, and this tendency was taken to a logical extreme in the omission of the word by one minuscule and the Sahidic (v).

If the story I have tried to reconstruct is right, the disruptive word was not, however, ἐνεστῶτος, but πονηροῦ. The fact that the present age is evil was assumed by Paul, and a glossator added the idea in the margin. From there the word was copied into the text, first of all in the wrong place (i). One minuscule, 1955, seems to have preserved the original text (vi).

1.6 omit Χριστου

The precise relation of Χριστοῦ to the rest of the sentence is puzzling. Jerome and Bengel construed the word with ἀπό, which is certainly possible, but it seems easier to take Χριστοῦ with ἐν χάριτι. Yet to specify the grace is to rob the sentence of its force, for the issue between Paul and those who are trying to make the Galatians change their mind is not *whether* they should be Christ's, but *how*. The word Χριστοῦ is read by p⁵¹ ℵ A B K P Ψ 33 81 1739 (D 326 read Ἰησοῦ Χριστοῦ), but three minuscules, 7 327 336, read θεοῦ, and p⁴⁶ᵛⁱᵈ F* G Marc Tert Cypr Ambst Victorin Pelag omit all additions to χάριτι. The shortest text is here the original (Zahn, Lietzmann, Oepke).

1.6 omit απο του καλεσαντος υμας εν χαριτι

If the shorter text argued for in the previous note is original, the possibility arises that by the one who called the Galatians Paul this time means himself rather than God or Christ. Of course he would understand that his call was the means by which God's call came to the Galatians (cf. 2 Thess. 2.14), but he could hardly mean that the defection or threatened defection of the Galatians from his teaching, serious as it was, was complete defection from God. He regarded Jews who failed to acknowledge Jesus Christ as still worshipping God, even if they did not wholly obey him (Rom. 10.2; cf. 9.4f). Bruno Bauer adduced the idea that defection from Paul's position was defection from God as evidence that the true author of Galatians was far removed from the time and circumstances of Paul.[1] I cite in support of the possibility that Paul here refers to his own preaching the sentence in Gal. 5.8: ἡ πεισμονὴ οὐκ ἐκ τοῦ καλοῦντος ὑμᾶς where it is possible that Paul referred to himself.[2] If Paul had meant in 1.6 that the Galatians were defecting from God, he would hardly have called that to which they were defecting εὐαγγέλιον, in however qualified a sense.

Nevertheless, it remains difficult to think that Paul would have written ἐν χάριτι if he himself were the one who called (cf. 1.15; Rom. 3.24 δικαιούμενοι δωρεὰν τῇ αὐτοῦ χάριτι). If God is meant, then I do not see how to avoid Bruno Bauer's objection, except by supposing either that the whole clause is an interpolation, or that the words ἐν χάριτι are an interpolation, or that the words ἐν χάριτι mean "to a situation of grace" (Lietzmann's first possibility, cf. 1 Cor. 7.15). The textual evidence in favour of the first hypothesis is that Ambrose (Psalm 40.38) omits the clause: miror quod sic tam cito transferimini in aliud euangelium, quod non est aliud, nisi aliqui sunt qui vos peruertunt. In favour of the third hypothesis is that Marcion and the Vulgate read εἰς χάριν. I am inclined to trust that Ambrose has preserved a genuine variant, and to argue that the whole clause was originally a gloss, modelled on 1.15, written by a scribe who understood the Galatians' defection as a defection from God.

1. *Kritik der paulinischen Briefe, Erste Abtheilung: Der Ursprung des Galaterbriefs* (Berlin 1850), p. 9.
2. See the comment on 5.11 below and the note. Henry Owen (1716–95) in W. Bowyer, *Critical Conjectures and Observations on the New Testament, Collected from*

Various Authors, As well in regard Words as Pointing: With the Reasons on which both are founded (3rd edn, much enlarged, ed. J. Nichols, with the help of Dr Owen, 1782), p. 365: "That τοῦ καλέσαντος ὑμᾶς must refer to the Apostle, and not to Christ, is evident from the 11th verse. And indeed, otherwise I known not well how the 8th and 9th could be inserted with any propriety."

1.7 omit ἄλλο

In what sense does ὃ οὐκ ἔστιν ἄλλο qualify ἕτερον εὐαγγέλιον? No doubt ἄλλο refers back to the preceding phrase and not on to the next clause, but how? If ἕτερος and ἄλλος were taken strictly so that ἕτερος meant a second of the same kind and ἄλλος another qualitatively different, we might expect ὃ ἔστιν ἄλλο: which is a different gospel altogether, not simply a second of the same kind. That is, if the two words are to be given their strict sense—and their closeness suggests that they must—Paul should have used ἄλλο the first time instead of ἕτερον. If, however, the strict distinction cannot be pressed, the contrast must turn on the word εὐαγγέλιον. In that case we might expect ὃ οὐκ ἔστιν ἄλλο εὐαγγέλιον: which is not a different gospel at all because it is not the gospel. This is the interpretation most commentators adopt. Unfortunately the contrast ends with ἄλλο. The emphasis must then lie on ἄλλο, and the meaning would be: which is not really different, because the gospel, in whatever form it comes, is always the same. Paul himself can scarcely have inserted such an irenic comment at this point, and the whole clause could be regarded as a gloss, as Baljon and Cramer regard it. However, I find difficulty in seeing why even a glossator would be so irrelevant.

The true solution seems to be that ἄλλο was originally a gloss against ἕτερον. The glossator was pointing out that Paul would have expressed his sentiments more clearly, in saying that the other gospel they had turned to was not really gospel at all, if he had used ἄλλο for ἕτερον. Paul seems to have appreciated the difference (cf. Gal. 5.10 and 2 Cor. 11.4: ἄλλον Ἰησοῦν . . . ἢ πνεῦμα ἕτερον . . . ἢ εὐαγγέλιον ἕτερον), but his point would have been spoilt, not made, if he had used ἄλλο for ἕτερον in this context. The good news now being preached to the Galatians seemed to be a variant of the good news they had accepted, but Paul begs leave to doubt whether it was as good as it sounded. He ends the next sentence (which loosely depends on θαυμάζω) by charging the trouble-makers with perverting the good news of Christ. The glossator was encouraged to make his point by supposing that

22

εὐαγγέλιον was a technical term denoting the agreed preaching of the Church, but Paul is not arguing on the grounds that these teachers were perverting what was standardized. He uses εὐαγγέλιον to mean good news, and argues that the news about Christ the others were bringing was not as good as they hoped to persuade the Galatians it was. When εὐαγγέλιον means "good news", ἕτερον fits beautifully, while leaving the way open for Paul to make the further point that the so-called "good news" is not what it seems, and is even a perversion of the good news of Christ.

Verses 6 and 7 as amended may be paraphrased like this. "I marvel that you are changing over so quickly to some other good news—which is not really good news at all. I would marvel, had there not been people who are disturbing you and wanting to pervert the good news of Christ."

1.10   omit η τον θεον

The verb πείθω always implies, as far as I can see, an effort by the subject to change the mind of the person in the object, and this even in cases where God is the object (Josephus, *Ant.* 4.123; 8.255, Ps. Clem. *Hom.* 3.64). No doubt, striving to persuade someone involves trying to please him, but the verb does not seem to *mean* this. As the question stands, it must mean, then, that Paul is asking himself whether he will persuade men to change their mind and follow his teaching, or whether he will persuade God to change his mind (as it were) and curse the men he had previously blessed; that is, Paul is asking himself whether or not to invoke the anathema he has been talking about in verses 8 and 9.

However, the context of the question is chiefly governed by what follows, not by what precedes. In the context of a further question, ἢ ζητῶ ἀνθρώποις ἀρέσκειν, the verb πείθω must be used in a bad sense: Am I now to cajole men? (ἄρτι refers to a possible future change of policy. γάρ is designed to emphasize how ridiculous it would be to suppose—as he has for the sake of the argument supposed in the previous two verses—that he would ever change his mind; for that would mean trying to please men rather than serve Christ; cf. γάρ in 1 Cor. 11.22, Oepke). But this interpretation leaves no room for a question about whether or not to persuade God. Any persuasion of God would be as a suppliant,

23

not as a cajoler (cf. 2 Cor. 5.11; 1 Thess. 2.4). The same verb could hardly govern such different objects in such different senses.

I therefore follow Weisse in taking the words ἢ τὸν θεόν as a gloss. The glossator possibly thought that Paul was wondering whether or not to continue with his appeal to the Galatians to hold back from heresy, and supposed that the alternative course of action was for Paul to appeal to God to reject them by invoking the anathema. He would have understood the next question as a third possibility, to give in to men and abandon his position. He read, "Shall I now persuade men (by continuing my appeals), or seek to please men (by giving up my position)?" and added after the first verb, "or shall I appeal to God (by calling down a curse)?" This interpretation of the two questions is unlikely to be right, not least because the "men" in each case would be different, in the first case the Galatians, and in the second the trouble-makers. But it is a plausible enough interpretation to suggest how the gloss came to be there at all. Whatever the reason for the gloss, the words are far easier to understand as a gloss than as part of the text.

The words *aut deo* are omitted by the twelfth or thirteenth-century Latin Codex Colbertinus (c), and this counts as slight textual evidence in favour of the conjecture.

omit *1.13, 14, 22–4*

These verses have been interpolated into Paul's argument by a later writer who wished to glorify the apostle. The argument is irrelevant and anachronistic, the concepts differ from Paul's concepts, and the vocabulary and style are not his.

Paul is arguing that he was directly commissioned by God, through a revelation of his Son, to spread the good news among the Gentiles. Although he visited Jerusalem to get information from Cephas,[1] and there saw James, the Lord's brother, he was not indebted to them for his special commission. That visit was three years after his call, and his first reaction to the call had not been to go to Jerusalem but to go to Arabia. What is at stake is his right to serve Christ as he has been called to serve him. The astounding reversal of roles he underwent, from a fierce persecutor of the Church to an evangelist of the faith, and from a precociously zealous Jew to an opponent of Jewish customs, is no argument in

24

favour of Paul's position. His position stands or falls on the revelation he has received and the recognition accorded him by the "pillars" in Jerusalem.

E. Bammel[2] has suggested that the trouble-makers in Galatia had attacked Paul because he had once been a persecutor of the Church, and that Paul was defending himself by admitting all, and then citing the praise of him that was used in the Judean churches:

$$\text{ὁ διώκων ἡμᾶς ποτε}$$
$$\text{νῦν εὐαγγελίζεται}$$
$$\text{τὴν πίστιν ἥν ποτε ἐπόρθει.}$$

It is hard to imagine the men who visited Galatia finding ammunition to use against Paul in his activities before he was called. Even if this were brought up against Paul, it is even harder to imagine that Paul would cite the approval of the Judean churches as support for his case. His case rested solely on the commission from God and the subsequent approval he received from the authorities who might otherwise have been thought of as his commissioners. What the Judean churches thought was neither here nor there. Paul had asked the Galatians ironically in verse 10 whether he should now try to please men, and he is not likely, a few sentences later, to quote the men he had pleased.

The interpolation is anachronistic because it regards Judaism as an entity distinct from Christianity.[3] Jews at the time used the term Ἰουδαϊσμός to describe their faith in opposition to heathenism (2 Macc. 2.21; 8.1; 14.38; 4 Macc. 4.26; synagogue inscription in Frey, C.I.J. I.694), but the use of the term in a Christian context seems to imply that Christianity is a system completely distinct from Judaism. Paul was well aware of the tragic gulf that had opened up between those Jews who believed in Jesus Christ and those who refused to believe, but he still held fast to the fact that "theirs were the fathers" (Rom. 9.5), that the fathers of those who believed in Christ were also the fathers of the unbelieving Jews. But this interpolation speaks in the terms to be found in the Apostolic Fathers of the second century, when Judaism had become a foreign entity (Ignatius *Magn.* 8.1; 10.3; *Philad.* 6.1).

The concepts employed are rarely found in Paul, or are entirely absent. In verse 23 πίστις is used of the Christian religion, as in Acts 6.7, and the only possible parallels in Paul are at 3.23–5, 6.10, and Rom. 1.5, all passages that are of doubtful authenticity.[4]

25

When verse 13 is read in conjunction with verse 23, it seems likely that ἐκκλησία is used in the first instance as the word for the Church as a whole; either the universal Church, or the Church of the Judean provinces. Although Paul was active as a persecutor only in Jerusalem, he planned to persecute Christians in Damascus; the destruction of Christian congregations everywhere is what is contemplated in the phrase καὶ ἐπόρθουν αὐτήν. The Judean churches which did not know him by sight regarded him as persecuting them.

But Paul almost always uses the word to refer to a local congregation.[5] He had an ideal opportunity to use the singular in 1.2, if that was his custom, but there he wrote ταῖς ἐκκλησίαις τῆς Γαλατίας. In 1 Thess. 2.14 he spoke of "the churches of God that are in Judea in Christ Jesus".[6]

The vocabulary of this section is unusual. The word ἀναστροφή occurs only in Ephesians and 1 Timothy among the books of the Pauline corpus, and Ἰουδαϊσμός, πορθέω, συνηλικιώτης, and πατρικός are not found elsewhere in that corpus. The enclitic ποτέ occurs three times here, once more in Galatians (at 2.6), and only nine times elsewhere in the Pauline corpus, excluding Ephesians and the Pastorals (where it occurs seven times).

The style of the section is even and steady, unlike the style of Paul. The sentences consist of 20, 19, 12, and 20 words respectively. καί joins distinct clauses with verbs in the indicative three times (1.13, 14, 24), which is rather frequent in comparison with the five times in the rest of the epistle (1.17, 18; 3.6 O.T.; 5.1; 6.2). The imperfect occurs seven times in this section, and only eight times elsewhere in the epistle (1.10 twice; 2.6; 2.12 twice; 3.23; 4.3, 29). Two of the imperfects are periphrastic, and we are told that the periphrastic construction was on the increase.[7]

The case for regarding 1.13, 14, 22, 23, 24 as an interpolation is a strong one as it stands, but to complete the case I must try to explain why anyone should wish to add this sort of note to Paul's text. E. Bammel has already shown that verse 23 probably contains a citation from a Judean church tradition, and I think it likely that this thesis can be extended to cover the whole of the section I have isolated. The author possessed Judean traditions about Paul, the persecutor who became the champion of the faith, and he inserted them into Galatians at the appropriate points in the story. His source was Judean as opposed to Jerusalemite,[8] so that he has to explain that, although they used to

26

say "He who once persecuted *us*", they did not know him by sight.

Because he was employing old traditions, the interpolator did not regard his additions as illegitimate. He saw himself as enriching a treasured epistle by an edifying reminiscence of the conversion of St Paul, which could appropriately be put onto his lips.

1. G. D. Kilpatrick, "Galatians 1:18 *ΙΣΤΟΡΗΣΑΙ ΚΗΦΑΝ*", *New Testament Essays: Studies in Memory of Thomas Walter Manson*, ed. A. J. B. Higgins (1959), pp. 144–9.
2. E. Bammel, "Galater 1.23", *ZNW* 59 (1968), pp. 108–12 at p. 111. The germ of the idea was first put forward by E. Barnikol, *Die vorchristliche und frühchristliche Zeit des Paulus, Forschungen zur Entstehung des Urchristentums des N.T. und der Kirche I* (Kiel 1929), p. 50.
3. Cf. Bruno Bauer, op. cit., p. 13.
4. Cf. E. Bammel, op. cit., p. 108, n. 1.
5. J. Y. Campbell, "The Origin and Meaning of the Christian Use of the word *ΕΚΚΛΗΣΙΑ*", *JTS* xlix (1948), pp. 130–42; reprinted in *Three New Testament Studies* (Leiden 1965), pp. 41–54. Excluding Ephesians, he argues that only in Col. 1.18, 24 it is beyond question that the word has a wider significance; in eight other instances that is more or less likely.
6. The phrase ἐδίωξα τὴν ἐκκλησίαν τοῦ θεοῦ in 1 Cor. 15.9 is parallel to our phrase in Gal. 1.13. It is possible that "God's church" in 1 Corinthians could refer to the congregation in Jerusalem, but the true solution seems to be that 1 Cor. 15.1–11 is a later credal summary not written by Paul.
7. Blass-Debrunner-Funk, §65(4).
8. Judea in v. 22 must exclude Jerusalem (Lightfoot against Lipsius; T. Mommsen, *ZNW* 2 (1901), p. 85; W. Heitmüller, *ZNW* 13 (1912), pp. 320ff).

2.2 omit αυτοις

The clause κατ' ἰδίαν δὲ τοῖς δοκοῦσιν can scarcely be taken as a closer definition of what was meant by αὐτοῖς (I laid the gospel before them, I mean privately before the pillars). In that case, the verb ἀνεθέμην would have had to be repeated (Oepke). Yet the more usual interpretation does not seem very satisfactory either. On this interpretation αὐτοῖς is rightly taken to refer to the Christians in Jerusalem, according to the convention that the pronoun would refer to the inhabitants of the previously named city (Schlier). Then the commentators argue that the clause we are discussing simply emphasized the private consultations which were held alongside the public congress (Lightfoot, Duncan, Schlier, Oepke). This reading seems very strained. The particle δέ loses all its adversative force, and would require to be translated "and also privately", which is scarcely possible. Further-more, the following clause has to be taken very unnaturally. If any phrase marked with δέ or ἀλλά occurs in a sentence followed by μή πως, that phrase would naturally signify the manner of acting adopted in order to guard against the fear mentioned in the μή πως clause. (1 Cor. 9.27: ἀλλὰ ὑπωπιάζω μου τὸ σῶμα . . . μή πως ἄλλοις κηρύξας αὐτὸς ἀδόκιμος γένωμαι; 2 Cor. 9.3f: ἔπεμψα δὲ τοὺς ἀδελφούς . . . μή πως ἐὰν ἔλθωσιν σὺν ἐμοὶ Μακεδόνες καὶ εὕρωσιν ὑμᾶς ἀπαρασκευάστους καταισχυνθῶμεν ἡμεῖς). The natural way to take the clause κατ᾽ ἰδίαν δὲ τοῖς δοκοῦσιν would be as the manner of consultation adopted by Paul to guard against the fear that he had run in vain. However, this interpretation requires us to understand that Paul did not lay the gospel before an open assembly at all. We should, therefore, accept the variant reading of the Codex Ψ (according to von Soden) and omit the word αὐτοῖς. The verb ἀνεθέμην may stand without an indirect object (2 Macc. 3.9; Acta Barnabae 4: Παῦλος δὲ ὁ ἀπόστολος οὐκ ἦν ἔγγιστα ἡνίκα ἀνεθέμην τὰ μυστήρια.)

The word αὐτοῖς could easily have been added. The verb might seem to require an indirect object straightaway, and the addition of αὐτοῖς would be in harmony with the public hearing implied in Acts 15.4. I can see no reason why a scribe would omit the word.

The verse should then be translated, "But I went up in obedience to revelation, and I submitted the gospel that I preach among the Gentiles, but to the authorities in private, lest I be running or had run in vain".

The interpretation I have adopted will have nothing to do with attempts to make the last clause into a purpose clause (Lipsius) or into an indirect question (Zahn, Oepke). The latter suggestion lacks convincing parallels, since 1 Thess. 3.5 fails to bear the required meaning (Frame, Schlier), and the former founders on the indicative ἔδραμον (cf. Gal. 4.11). The commentators who adopt the natural sense of the clause, and take it to refer to the apostle's fear, try to avoid the implication that Paul himself is afraid of anything. They suppose that the words "must be taken to express his fear lest the Judaic Christians, by insisting on the Mosaic ritual, might thwart his past and present endeavours to establish a Church on a liberal basis" (Lightfoot). This strained interpretation is required because the commentators relate the last clause to the very act of submitting the gospel, but the reading

I have adopted relates the last clause to the privacy of the consultation. The apostle submitted the gospel privately, in case he was running in vain.

The tortuous interpretation cited from Lightfoot, and followed by most commentators, seems necessary in order to avoid a blank denial of all that Paul has been insisting on in the first chapter of the epistle. If his commission was given by God and if he made no attempt to please men, he could not have admitted to asking the Jerusalem leaders to tell him whether or not he was in the right. Yet we cannot deny that the whole of this second chapter of the epistle portrays the Jerusalem leaders as authorities exercising a quasi-judicial power. As Lightfoot shrewdly notes, to his own discomfort, the natural drift of verse 2 is "slightly favoured by οὐδὲν προσανέθεντο, ver. 6".

I think the seeming contradiction can be resolved if we distinguish between Paul's commission from God, which is irrevocable and unchangeable, and the test of fruitfulness. When Paul first went to preach to the Gentiles his mission might have been unsuccessful. It was not unsuccessful, for the Galatians, among others, responded and believed, but he might then also have run in vain. Now he goes to Jerusalem according to revelation to submit his work to a second test of success, and this test might also have failed, without calling into question his original commission. He would presumably have had to conclude that God's time was not yet ripe.

But what can be the point of submitting to the judgement of the Jerusalem apostles if the judgement did not concern the very thing that Paul has insisted in chapter 1 was beyond human judgement, his preaching to the Gentiles? What else can the Jerusalem apostles be deciding than that Paul has been right or wrong from the very beginning? They were deciding, I believe, no such general issue, but simply the concrete particular issue whether they, as the leaders of Israel that had acknowledged her Messiah, would accept the Gentiles who had also acknowledged Jesus as Messiah, but without becoming proselytes, as the first-fruits of the obedience of the Gentiles which had been promised. Had they decided not to accept Paul's work, Paul would have known that his race had been in vain. This would have been a staggering blow to him, meaning that Israel was not yet ready to accept one of the promised messianic signs, but the blow could not strike at his personal commission from God.

Paul deliberately sought private audience so that, if the authorities were not yet ready to accept the Gentiles, the refusal would not have been public, and Paul would not have had to labour against the disappointment the Gentile Christians would have inevitably suffered at their first rebuff. He would have continued to work for a response from the Gentiles, and he would have continued to hope for an acceptance of these Gentiles by the representatives of Israel, the leaders in Jerusalem.

What was the content of this commission, which hitherto we have described generally as the commission to preach to the Gentiles? We must now be more precise. The commission was to preach Jesus Christ to the Gentiles without at the same time asking that they become Jews. That commission Paul could never give up to please men, but at the same time that commission had to be carried out, had to be submitted to the test of history, and could have proved, for the time being, fruitless. The first test was successful, and the Gentiles began to believe. The second test might have been unsuccessful, but it too succeeded. The representatives of Israel acknowledged Paul's work, did not compel Titus to be circumcised, and laid no conditions (unless the request for financial help be a condition) on the Gentile congregations through Paul their representative.

2.3 omit Τίτος

This is an extraordinary sentence, and yet it is not to be lightened, except perhaps in one small particular, by supposing that it has been glossed. The one feature of the sentence which needs attention is the phrase Τίτος ὁ σὺν ἐμοί. The Chester Beatty Papyrus omits ὁ σὺν ἐμοί and the Codex Vaticanus omits the article ὁ. In view of the observation that Paul had Titus with him in verse 1, we might well regard ὁ σὺν ἐμοί as superfluous, and therefore a gloss. This is the reading of p[46], but I hesitate to regard it as the original, on the grounds that there is no conceivable reason why a later scribe should have regarded the gloss as required. No one could have doubted that the Titus who was not compelled to be circumcised was the very same Titus whom Paul brought with him, verse 1. The fact that B perhaps finds difficulty with the grammatical form of the phrase, and omits the article, indicates that ὁ σὺν ἐμοί belonged to the earliest text. In that case, the really

30

superfluous word could be Τίτος. It is easy to see how the name could have been added to the text. The original may well have been, ἀλλ᾿ οὐδὲ ὁ σὺν ἐμοί, Ἕλλην ὤν, ἠναγκάσθη περιτμηθῆναι, "But not even my companion, who is a Greek, was compelled to be circumcised".

What, then, does the sentence imply?

Two things seem to be assumed: one, that the Jerusalem authorities would have had the legitimate power to compel Titus to be circumcised had they so decided (not of course power to compel the circumcision by the exercise of force, but moral power which Paul recognized as legitimate); and the other—but here I am less certain—that, had Titus been compelled to be circumcised, Paul's argument that Gentile Christians as a whole need not be circumcised would not necessarily have failed. The second assumption seems to be implied in the expression οὐδέ, "not even my companion, who is a Greek". The "not even" might be taken to suggest that one would expect all the members and visitors of the congregations who acknowledged Jesus as Messiah in Jerusalem to be Jews.

If these assumptions be correct, Paul's argument takes on compelling power. If Titus was brought (perhaps deliberately, for this very reason)[1] into the ambit of the Jerusalem church; if this church had spiritual authority to circumcise him; and if that circumcision would not necessarily have destroyed Paul's case that his Gentile congregations should remain Gentile, then the proof is overwhelming that Jerusalem has recognized Paul's mission.

1. The risk may not have been very great. Paul perhaps knew that the Jerusalem church had taken a decision not to circumcise Gentile converts. The "Jerusalem Decree" of Acts 15.28–9 (cf. 15.20; 21.25) had perhaps already been made.

2.4, 5, 6 4 omit δε
5 omit οις; omit ινα η αληθεια του ευαγγελιου διαμεινη προς υμας
6 omit δε

These three verses raise a tangle of textual, grammatical, and exegetical problems. I wish to put forward a speculative solution to the problems, and in justification plead that such a speculative solution at least explains the difficulties without recourse to the hypothesis that the apostle lapsed from clarity at just the point in this argument where clarity was imperatively required.

The great difficulty in verse 4 is to decide the reference of the first phrase. The use of the particle δέ would seem to throw the reference forward, because there is no clear indication in the previous clause of what is being qualified. Nor is it likely that one sentence would contain two qualifications indicated by δέ: οὐδὲ (Τίτος) ὁ σὺν ἐμοί and διὰ δὲ τοὺς ψευδαδέλφους. If δέ throws the reference forward, we must then, perhaps, suppose that the main idea has been omitted, an idea like "the leading Apostles urged me to yield" (Lightfoot). But Paul was not averse to recounting a conflict with a leading apostle—see verse 14 of this same chapter—and it is hard to understand why he should omit an account of a quarrel which, on this hypothesis, he won.

The other possibility, on the supposition that δέ throws the reference forward, is to take the phrase with the verb εἴξαμεν. That is the most natural construction when the words οἷς οὐδέ are omitted. Verse 5 without οἷς οὐδέ pretty clearly refers to the case of Timothy in Acts 16. (It can scarcely imply, as some modern commentators have argued, but no ancient commentators, that Paul did circumcise Titus, not under compulsion but willingly.) Acts 16.3 explains that Paul λαβὼν περιέτεμεν αὐτὸν διὰ τοὺς Ἰουδαίους τοὺς ὄντας ἐν τοῖς τόποις ἐκείνοις. The διά-phrase in Gal. 2.4 would therefore almost inevitably be related to the verb εἴξαμεν by a scribe who adopted the shorter reading.

However, as I shall argue later, it is most unlikely that we should accept the shorter reading as the original. In that case we must ask whether the one word which relates the διά-phrase forward, the δέ, is a true part of the text. The word δέ is omitted by Marcion, with the support from Jerome and the Antiochenes, Theodore of Mopsuestia and Severian. Without the particle, the whole phrase goes easily with the preceding verb: "for not even my companion who was a Greek was compelled to be circumcised on account of the false intruding[1] brothers who came in to spy out the freedom we have in Christ Jesus". The intruders must have been intruders into the church at Antioch, otherwise we should have to suppose, on the previous argument, that they managed to penetrate into the private meeting between Paul, Barnabas, and Titus with the "pillars" in Jerusalem. But then there would be nothing to "spy out"; the meeting was openly concerned with the issue. This description of the false brothers must apply to their activities away in the churches from which Paul has come. The sense of verses 3 and 4 is that the pressure brought by these agitators was not sufficient to lead even to the requirement that a Greek received by the Jerusalem congregation be circumcised, much less that Greeks in a Greek environment be circumcised.

2.5 The ἵνα-clause needs examination. The first suspicious circumstance is the use of the subjunctive διαμείνῃ. Certainly ἵνα with the subjunctive occurs without question in Galatians at 1.16; 2.10; 2.16; 3.14b; 3.22; 3.24; 4.5 twice, but there are four cases where the indicative is used in at least some manuscripts, and one case where the form itself is ambiguous. The ambiguous case is in 2.19 (future indicative or aorist subjunctive), and the four uncertain cases (with manuscript support for the indicative given in brackets) are: 2.4 (א A B* C D 326; middle, L 309); 3.14a (440); 3.14b (642); 4.17 (almost the whole ms. tradition); 6.13 (D G* P 47*vid 114 116). It is reasonable to suppose that Paul used the indicative, which was changed sporadically by scribes thinking to correct his grammar. But the close conjunction of an almost certainly original indicative in 2.4 with an unchallenged subjunctive in 2.5 may be an indication that the latter instance is the work of a glossator who naturally employed the subjunctive.

The second suspicious circumstance is that the ἵνα-clause in the sentence as it stands is a little inconsequential. The emphasis on "not even for an hour" in the main clause would lead us to expect a *negative* ἵνα-clause: "not even for an hour have we yielded, in order that the truth of the gospel be not taken from you" (in the lapse of even an hour). Perhaps the inconsequence would disappear if we supposed that Titus was in fact circumcised, and that Paul wished to assert this event was not a matter of principle. Then the emphasis would fall on τῇ ὑποταγῇ, and we should have to understand the sentence like this: "To them we have not yielded for an hour on the subjection issue (though we may have for the sake of peace circumcised Titus), in order that the truth of the gospel might remain with you" (cf. Duncan). However, there are no grounds in verse 4 for supporting that Titus was circumcised, and this way of taking verse 5 is, in any case, highly artificial.

The inconsequence completely disappears when we omit the negative, οὐδέ, from the main clause: "we yielded for an hour to subjection in order that the truth of the gospel might remain

33

continually with you". The subordinate clause explains that the temporary concession was designed to gain a lasting benefit.

We have already argued that the shorter text had in mind the case of Timothy, and the whole of Acts would lend support to the supposition that, if Timothy's circumcision was a concession, it led to a remarkable gain for the Gentile Christians who, by Paul's willingness to meet Jewish scruples, got the support of the Jerusalem church for their evangelization.

However, this reading of the history is not accurate, nor, indeed, entirely fair to the Book of Acts. As Acts makes clear, Paul did not circumcise Timothy as an act of submission. Timothy was by law a Jew, and the circumcision in no way prejudiced the principle that Gentile converts were not to be circumcised.[2] It follows that the text without the negative οὐδέ cannot be the work of Paul, for he would never have argued that the case of Timothy was relevant to the issue at stake in Galatians. The word οὐδέ belonged to Paul's original text.

Therefore I conclude that the ἵνα-clause was a gloss to an emended text, for strictly speaking it follows only from the shorter secondary statement that Paul yielded for an hour. Marcion does not cite the ἵνα-clause, but nor does he cite verses 6–9a, so that we cannot conclude that the clause was lacking in his text.[3]

When the words in the subordinate clause are omitted, we are confronted by an entirely new possibility. The opening words of verse 6, ἀπὸ δὲ τῶν δοκούντων εἶναί τι, are universally regarded as a false start to the sentence at the end of the same verse, ἐμοὶ γὰρ οἱ δοκοῦντες οὐδὲν προσανέθεντο; "the sentence, which was begun in ἀπὸ . . . εἶναί τι and then broken off by the parenthesis, is here resumed, but in a different form" (Lightfoot). Certainly, the particle δέ assumes that this is the case, but the particle δέ is omitted by the minuscule 33, and could well be an addition to make the best of a bad text.

The new possibility is that these words at the beginning of verse 6 are the genuine conclusion to the sentence in verse 5.

Before I can attempt to justify this possibility, however, I have to discuss the word οἷς at the beginning of verse 5. It is commonly argued that this must be original, since no scribe would have inserted a word which created an anacolouthon. Against that I argue that the οἷς was first inserted (perhaps an an alternative to οὐδέ) when the previous verse still lacked its particle δέ and was still (rightly) regarded as the conclusion of verse 3. When verse 4 was read with verse 3, οἷς would be a reasonable emendation of οὐδέ for a scribe who assumed that Paul would have had to explain the case of Timothy's circumcision in this context. This scribe would regard verse 6 as a unit in which οἱ δοκοῦντες in both cases were the same men. The reading οἷς without οὐδέ is witnessed to by Jerome, Primasius, and Sedulius as occurring in some Latin manuscripts.

On this argument, the text of Marcion, the Syriac Peshitta, Ephraem, and Greek codices according to the Ambrosiaster, which reads οὐδὲ πρὸς ὥραν, was the original.

The shortest reading, omitting οὐδέ as well, is found in D*, Irenaeus (Latin), Tertullian, Ambrosiaster, Pelagius. This I should explain as a straight emendation to deal with the case of Timothy. It is compatible with any of the possible ways of taking the surrounding sentences.

The original text of verses 3–6 I conjecture was as follows:

4 ἀλλ' οὐδὲ ὁ σὺν ἐμοί, Ἕλλην ὤν, ἠναγκάσθη περιτμηθῆναι διὰ
   τοὺς παρεισάκτους ψευδαδέλφους οἵτινες παρεισῆλθον κατασκο-
   πῆσαι τὴν ἐλευθερίαν ἡμῶν ἣν ἔχομεν ἐν Χριστῷ Ἰησοῦ ἵνα
5 ἡμᾶς καταδουλώσουσιν. οὐδὲ πρὸς ὥραν εἴξαμεν τῇ ὑποταγῇ
6 ἀπὸ τῶν δοκούντων εἶναί τι. ὁποῖοί ποτε ἦσαν οὐδέν μοι δια-
   φέρει. πρόσωπον ὁ θεὸς ἀνθρώπου οὐ λαμβάνει. ἐμοὶ γὰρ οἱ
   δοκοῦντες οὐδὲν προσανέθεντο . . .

The sense of the newly recovered sentence in verses 5, 6a is, "not for an hour have we yielded to subjection from those reputed to be something". The preposition ἀπό denotes the origin of the action implied by the noun, and the article τῇ, which has always puzzled commentators (Schlier), is required by the construction.

It is now clear that οἱ δοκοῦντες εἶναί τι, which is a standard phrase with a derogatory sense (cf. 6.3; Plato *Ap.* 41E; *Euthyd.* 303C; *Gorg.* 472A), cannot refer to the same people as οἱ δοκοῦντες in 2.2 and 6b or οἱ δοκοῦντες στῦλοι εἶναι in 9. The context of these latter occurrences shows that Paul is speaking respectfully and gratefully of men he regards as wielding lawful authority. At the beginning of verse 6, on the other hand, we can now see that he is describing the false brothers who have been claiming an authority God does not recognize. Human position does not count in God's sight, and Paul refuses to be cowed by the authority they claim on the basis of their former status.

35

The history of this passage possibly went like this.

Scribes who did not recognize the entire difference between οἱ δοκοῦντες and οἱ δοκοῦντες εἶναί τι took verse 6 as an interrupted and broken sentence, and inserted a particle at the beginning. This separation was made almost irrevocable when the last clause of verse 5, a gloss to the inferior shorter text of verse 5, was incorporated into the passage. The negative was omitted from verse 5 in order to make the sentence refer to Timothy's circumcision. The relative οἷς was an insertion or even an emendation made when verse 4 was still regarded as the conclusion to the sentence in verse 3. The particle δέ at the beginning of verse 4 was inserted to relate verse 4 to verse 5 in its shortest form, without οἷς οὐδέ.

It will be objected that on my hypothesis all of the best manuscripts, with the exception of D, contain contrary textual features; B, for example, reads δέ in verse 4, and οἷς in verse 5, οὐδέ at the beginning of verse 5 and the ἵνα-clause at the end. Only Marcion reads anything approaching the supposed original text, omitting δέ in verse 4, οἷς in verse 5, and not reading the ἵνα-clause in verse 5. Only D offers a consequentially emended text, with δέ in verse 4, no οἷς οὐδέ in verse 5, a ἵνα-clause to round off the matter of Timothy, and a δέ at the beginning of verse 6 to mark the beginning of an anacolouthon.

The objection is that we might well expect that more texts than Marcion and D would exhibit consequential texts. My answer is that scribes would on the whole prefer to transcribe the longest text, being unwilling to lose anything precious. Every addition would tend to be recorded, even if the addition depended for its sense on an omission that the scribe was not willing to adopt. This means that Vaticanus in fact bears traces of the whole history of the text. That history cannot, however, be read from Vaticanus, without evidence from other manuscripts that have gone a different way. My reading of the history is certainly speculative, but it is not vulnerable to the objection that different branches of the story are sometimes incompatibly present in the one manuscript.

The main defence of my reconstruction is that it offers an intelligible explanation of diverse textual variants, and that it recovers an original reading which both explains the later variants and rescues Paul's logic and clarity. Paul may have been wrong, but it is not likely that he would have been shuffling and evasive in an issue of such importance.

1. See Burton's note, p. 78, for the argument that the passive force should not be pressed.
2. For a fuller discussion see J. C. O'Neill, *The Theology of Acts in its Historical Setting* (2nd edn, 1970), pp. 104–5.
3. Harnack, *Marcion: Das Evangelium vom fremden Gott*, T.U. 45 (2nd edn, 1924, repr. Darmstadt 1960), p. 71* argues that Marcion must have had the ἵνα-clause in his text because "the truth of the Gospel was a central idea". But the phrase occurs in Gal. 2.14.

2.7, 8 7 omit καθως Πετρος της περιτομης
8 omit Πετρω

Paul always uses the name Κηφᾶς, except in Gal. 2.7, 8. Κηφᾶς appears in verse 9 as the second name in the list of the pillars (according to the most probable reading), and it is very difficult to see any motive for using a Greek form in the earlier part of the sentence, or for putting the man second in the list of three after giving him such prominence before. I conjecture that the phrase, καθὼς Πέτρος τῆς περιτομῆς and the word Πέτρῳ were originally glosses to the text, designed to incorporate the view, which we find in Matthew's Gospel, that Peter was the leader of the Jewish Church, into the picture presented by Galatians. The rest of Galatians does not support this picture. Not only does Cephas's name appear second in the list of the three pillars, but Cephas seems to have been subject to James in the matter of eating with Gentiles (2.12). In the Acts of the Apostles as well, James has much more authority in the Jewish congregations than Peter.

The phrase καθὼς Πέτρος τῆς περιτομῆς is omitted by K. There is no evidence in the manuscripts for the omission of Πέτρῳ, except perhaps in the old Latin S (Cambridge, Trinity College B. 10. 5), where the omission was self-corrected.

2.12 omit τινας; read ηλθεν for ηλθον

The present text seems to offer a straightforward picture of what happened in Antioch. Cephas came to Antioch; he ate with Gentile Christians; messengers arrived from James; Cephas withdrew from eating with Gentiles and persuaded his fellow-Jews to follow his example; Paul withstood him to his face. But, even on the present text, there are difficulties. Why does Paul say "When Cephas came to Antioch" if the scandal arose only after he had been there a little time? What use is it to oppose Cephas if James is the one behind the change of policy? If James prompted the change, why is Cephas's fear of the Jews given as the reason for the change?

If the present text raises difficulties of interpretation, these difficulties are not removed when we observe that a number of key words are read differently by p⁴⁶, ℵ, B, and D. But these various readings do suggest that our exegetical difficulties may have arisen because the original text has been corrupted in one way or another.

The chief various readings in verse 12 are as follows:

τινας   ℵ A B C D F G Ψ 33 330 451 2492 &c.; τινα   p⁴⁶ d gᶜ r*
ἦλθον   A C Dᶜ Ψ &c.; ἦλθεν   p⁴⁶ ℵ B D* F G 33 330 451 2492 d g r*

At first sight it might be assumed that the second variant was simply consequent upon the first: one messenger came from James and, when he came, Cephas withdrew from eating with Gentiles. However, that supposition will not explain that the first variant has very much less support than the second. It is far more likely that the first variant was a change made to bring the text into line with the second. The harder original text, which explains all the rest, is the text with τινας and ἦλθεν.

If the second sentence in verse 12 began ὅτε δὲ ἦλθεν, the verb must refer to Cephas, since Cephas is undoubtedly the subject of the main verbs of the sentence. This opening runs parallel to the opening of the sentence in verse 11, and lends support to the presumption, raised by that beginning, that Cephas decided to change his policy as soon as he arrived in Antioch.

Origen, however, took the singular as a reference to James:

ὅτι Πέτρος ἔτι φοβούμενος τοὺς Ἰουδαίους, παυσάμενος τοῦ μετὰ τῶν ἐθνῶν συνεσθίειν, ἐλθόντος Ἰακώβου πρὸς αὐτὸν ἀφώριζεν ἑαυτὸν κτλ. (contra Celsum II.1 [386]).

I cannot see how he would have come to this conclusion if his text had earlier read πρὸ τοῦ γὰρ ἐλθεῖν τινα/τινας ἀπὸ Ἰακώβου, and I conjecture that his text read πρὸ τοῦ γὰρ ἐλθεῖν τὸν Ἰάκωβον. This reading can hardly have been correct, since then Paul would have been forced to confront James himself, or at least explain why he did not confront James.

I think the solution might be that τινας was the remark of a glossator who wished to suggest that Peter was not responsible for this change of policy, but that responsibility lay with James, who by now was a figure of no significance in the hagiography of the Church.

Naber has already suggested that the whole phrase τινας ἀπὸ 'Ιακώβου was the gloss, but, attractive as this conjecture is, I find it hard to see any motive for the glossator's addition.

If the original text was as I have supposed, we no longer have to wonder about the connection between the arrival of messengers from James and Cephas's fear of "those of the circumcision". Cephas's fear of the Jews at Antioch now stands out as the main reason why he changed his policy of eating with Gentiles when he arrived in that city. Perhaps the clause πρὸ τοῦ γὰρ ἐλθεῖν ἀπὸ 'Ιακώβου refers to a visit he made to James before coming to Antioch, but it is possible that it conveys just the opposite impression and means that before he left James he used always to eat with Gentiles. James was strong enough to stand up to Jewish pressure, but Cephas was not; when he left James, Cephas succumbed.

2.14 omit εθνικως και ουκ

The first accusing question Paul says he asked Cephas is full of difficulties. "If you being a Jew live in the Gentile manner and not in the Jewish manner, how do you compel Gentiles to judaize?"

There are at least two problems. First, it is not at all certain that the act of eating with Gentiles automatically meant that a Jew ceased to be a Jew. In the dispersion the customs were laxer than in Palestine among strict Jews.[1] If Cephas had all along wished to remain a faithful Jew, he must have known it to be possible for a faithful Jew to eat with Gentiles, and we have no evidence that he ever wished to abandon this status as a Jew; his original decision to eat with Gentiles cannot have been a decision to abandon the Law. The matter must have been one for discussion among the rabbis, and Cephas's change of policy must reflect the current state of uncertainty about the issue.

Paul, of course, may have judged Cephas from the strictest Pharisaic point of view according to which any contact with Gentiles would defile. But this raises the second difficulty. If Paul was arguing that the only consistent and proper Judaism was his own previous strict position, Peter would have had not *one* but

39

two easy answers to Paul's charge. The first would be that he had never gone Gentile in a sense that most Jews would take seriously. The second would be that, if he had gone Gentile, he was now changing his policy and conforming to the best precepts of Pharisaic Judaism. He had admitted his past lapse, so that his past lapse could not be held against him if he were now indeed compelling the Gentiles to judaize. Paul's present tense ζῇς would be no longer true.

The logic of this sentence, on the face of it so simple, turns out to be very obscure, and all too easy for Cephas to answer, if he could have seen the point. Furthermore, Paul cannot have meant, If you have become to all intents a Gentile, how can you compel Gentiles to become Jews?, because he immediately goes on to emphasize that he and Cephas remain φύσει 'Ιουδαῖοι (verse 15). One moment he assumes that Cephas has gone Gentile, and asks him to draw the necessary conclusion; and the next moment he assumes that Cephas is a Jew.

In fact, the text of the question in verse 14 is in disarray, but I think we are given enough clues to be able to reconstruct a text which well introduces the following argument, and which is an opening salvo worthy of the debater Paul must have been.

The variants with which we are concerned are the following:

καὶ οὐκ 'Ιουδαϊκῶς   omit p⁴⁶ 917 d Victorin Ambst
καὶ   omit 206 1739
οὐκ   omit 429 (according to Tischendorf) 642* (Lambeth Palace 1185) 1522 (Lambeth Palace 1184) and according to von Soden: 639 1827 1845 2127 2298
ζῇς   before καὶ οὐκ 'Ιουδαϊκῶς   D K L 1908 vgᶜˡ syr

The first variant might seem to be a simple case of homoio-teleuton, did not the other variants suggest that something more was amiss. If we suppose that a gloss consisting of the words καὶ οὐκ 'Ιουδαϊκῶς has been added to the text for clarity's sake, we have not accounted for the curious fact that some minuscules omit οὐκ. It is more likely that the single word 'Ιουδαϊκῶς was the gloss. When we contemplate this possibility, we see that the supposed gloss would make very much better sense than the word it is glossing. Paul's question would then be, If you being a Jew live like a Jew, how do you compel Gentiles to live like Jews? We must examine the possibility, I think, that the real gloss was ἐθνικῶς, and the text was εἰ σὺ 'Ιουδαῖος ὑπάρχων 'Ιουδαϊκῶς ζῇς.

The gloss would be made by a scribe who thought Paul was arguing from Cephas's former practice of eating with Gentiles, and who (wrongly) thought, on the basis of his knowledge of Judaism after the fall of Jerusalem, that this was to "go Gentile". The gloss would have been substituted for the word Ἰουδαϊκῶς by some later scribes, while others would have incorporated the gloss into the text with what they regarded as the necessary emendation.

This conjecture does not run up against the historical difficulties which the usual text encounters. Whether or not Cephas ate with Gentiles he would be still living like a Jew; this was an open issue, while Cephas had not otherwise abandoned the marks of a Jew. He was applying strong pressure on the Gentile Christians to judaize, however, by withdrawing from the table-fellowship he had previously practised, and so suggesting that they would have to change their way of life drastically if table-fellowship were to be restored.

Although the conjecture passes these tests, it cannot be accepted until it can be shown to provide Paul with a fitting argument, and an argument which suits the context.

The argument would be, "If a Jew, because of his Jewish nature, has a right to live like a Jew, has not a Gentile also the right to be allowed to live as a Gentile?" The whole of the Old Testament could certainly be quoted in support of that principle. The only objection to it would be that righteousness depended on being a Jew and observing the Law. But Paul is able to meet this possible objection from Cephas by appealing in verses 15 and 16 to the fact, agreed by them both, that a man is not justified by the Law, but only by faith in Christ. Therefore, although the Law has preserved Jews from being sinners like the Gentiles, it has not produced the righteousness that alone would justify a Jew's putting pressure on Gentiles to become Jews. Cephas is fully entitled to live like a Jew, but he has no right to compel Gentiles to abandon their own status, since the way to righteousness does not lie through the Law. A corollary would be that any Gentile who wished to become a proselyte might do so, but no pressure should be applied by those who believed in Jesus Christ.

Some commentators assume that Paul is demanding that Cephas give up the Law entirely. Lipsius, for example, says, "Paul now goes right against the Jewish Christians in that he advocates the fundamental lifting of commitment to the Law even for Jewish

Christians, going quite beyond the terms of the agreement." He is right to say that the terms of the agreement did not involve the Jerusalem leaders in abandoning the Law, but he is wrong to suppose that the argument with Cephas implies a more radical shift in Paul's own position. The words ἐὰν μή in verse 16 show that Paul is not expecting Cephas to give up his living as a Jew, apart from the fact that this is the clear assumption behind the opening question in verse 14 as I have conjectured it should read. The Law has saved Jews from becoming sinners like the Gentiles, but its works have not, as the Psalmist said (Ps. 143.2), made any one righteous.

The conjectured question in verse 14 is based on textual evidence and seems to provide Paul with a good opening argument, which fits the context.

1. (Hermann L. Strack and) Paul Billerbeck, *Kommentar zum N.T. aus Talmud und Midrasch*, vol. iii (Munich 1926), pp. 421–2; vol. iv (1928), pp. 374–8.

2.17 omit the verse

The attempts to show the connection between verse 17, the preceding verses, and the following verse are legion. The argument in verse 17 is usually taken to be an argument about whether or not to abandon the Law. Lightfoot's setting out of the possibilities is still the clearest. The statement "Christ is minister of sin" is either a logical conclusion from a premiss which Paul wished to show up as false (or which the Jewish Christians were advancing), or the statement "Christ is minister of sin" is the illogical conclusion from a premiss which Paul wished to maintain as correct. In the first case the argument of Paul is this:

> To seek to be justified in Christ is to abandon the Law;
> to abandon the Law is sin;
> then Christ is minister of sin (which is absurd);
> therefore it is not sin to abandon the Law.

In the second case Paul's argument is this:

> To seek to be justified in Christ is to abandon the Law;
> to abandon the Law is to be found sinners;
> from which it does not follow that Christ is minister of sin
>   because there is no other way to be justified than to admit to

being a sinner: "We Jews look down upon the Gentiles as sinners: yet we have no help for it but to become sinners like them" (Lightfoot).

Both these interpretations are too complicated and subtle. There is no indication in the verse itself that the issue is the abandonment of the Law. The commentators have to draw that inference from the context but, as we have seen, the context in verses 15 and 16 does not at all clearly imply that to be a Christian requires the abandonment of the Law.

If we read the verse for its own sake without trying to connect it with the context, the issue is relatively simple. The issue concerns Christians who still sin although they are seeking to be justified in and through Christ. To be justified in Christ is ultimately to be sinless; yet Christians do commit sins. Has then Christ failed, and led to sin rather than to righteousness? Of course not!

This is a general theological problem which the Church always has to face, but it is hard to see what direct relevance the treatment of the problem here could have had in the tense meeting between Paul and Cephas. Verse 17 is possibly a later gloss.

The occasion for the gloss can be seen to be provided by verse 18, when verse 18 is taken as a general maxim governing the Christian life. As a general maxim, verse 18 states that, if a Christian begins to destroy the Christian character he has been building up, he proves himself a transgressor. The gloss comments that the real failures of Christians do not invalidate the claim that Christ is the servant of righteousness.

But was verse 18 originally meant to be a general maxim? No. I think that verse 18 was part of Paul's public accusation of Cephas, tactfully phrased in the first person singular.

Cephas had previously taken up a possible concessive interpretation of the Law in order to eat with his fellow Gentile Christians. He had begun to destroy the old necessary barrier between Jew and Gentile, and so to show that the messianic age had dawned, in which the Gentiles would gather with the Jews to worship God. Cephas had not broken the Law, at least on a more lenient interpretation, but had within his own position broken down one of the signs of the pre-messianic age that was passing away. Cephas's transgression or, as it is called in verse 13, his hypocrisy, was to step back into a more rigorous interpretation of

43

the Law and in practice to seem to question the recognition granted in Jerusalem to Paul's Gentile congregations.[1]

Commentators have often wondered why Paul does not claim or report a victory over Cephas. I think the reason is that the victory has already been reported in the favourable judicial decision at Jerusalem. Cephas's change of previous policy when he came to Antioch in no way reversed the Jerusalem decision, but it was a clear transgression against God in that it rebuilt barriers which had rightly been broken down by Cephas between the two parts of human creation, the Jews and the Gentiles. Paul's argument was compelling, and he could leave it at that. He is reporting his argument with Cephas to the Galatians in order to show that as Gentiles they have their proper acknowledged place besides the Jews in God's economy of salvation. Paul shows that he was not afraid to stand up to Cephas—whose authority as one of the "pillars" he has already acknowledged—in order to show Cephas that he was a transgressor. How much more should the Galatians stand up to men without any such authority who try to persuade the Gentiles to give up their status as the Gentile part of God's economy in the messianic age.

1. There is much to be said for Schmithal's suggestion that Paul was attacking Cephas's inconsistency rather than implying that Cephas would necessarily from the beginning have had to eat with the Gentile Christians. *Paulus und Jakobus* (Göttingen 1963), pp. 59f; *Paul and James* (1965), p. 72.

2.20 omit ζω δε ουκετι εγω
     ζη δε εν εμοι χριστος
omit του υιου

The first person singular in verse 18 was probably a rhetorical device adopted by Paul to accuse Cephas without offending him. The principle is put in the first person in order to show that it applies to any Christian. This device continued to the end of verse 21. Paul is confessing his own position, but at the same time he assumes that Cephas will share his assumptions and draw the same conclusions.

The only serious textual disturbance in this section is to be found at the end of verse 20. In place of the received text, τοῦ υἱοῦ τοῦ θεοῦ, which is supported by ℵ A C Dᶜ K L P Ψ 33 &c., a number of important manuscripts, p⁴⁶ B D* F G d g, read τοῦ θεοῦ καὶ

44

Χριστοῦ. It is hard to see how either of these readings could have been changed into the other, but it is possible that both are modifications of a common original. If the original text had been simply τοῦ θεοῦ, scribes would have felt obliged to ask themselves whether or not a mistake had occurred, since he who gives himself would seem to be Christ the Son and not the Father (Rom. 8.32; Eph. 5.2, 25). I am not sure that they would have been right. God who does not spare his Son could well be said to give himself for me. Burton's objection that the apostle nowhere speaks of faith in God is not quite correct, although I freely admit he speaks of faith in Christ immediately above (2.16). Paul's argument from Abraham would seem to entail that faith in God is a possible way of speaking. Faith in God who loved me and gave himself for me and faith in Christ would not be mutually exclusive. The verb παραδίδωμι is used with God as the implied subject in Rom. 4.25.

One minuscule, 330, reads τοῦ θεοῦ alone.

Whatever decision we take on this teasing textual problem, the surrounding argument is reasonably clear. God has bestowed a gift, which is not to be set aside, in giving Christ up to die. That gift allowed men to become righteous by faith, by complete trust. The fact that Christ had to die shows that righteousness was not attainable through the Law.

If this is the argument, the words ὃ δὲ νῦν ζῶ ἐν σαρκί must refer to the whole life of the Christian until he dies; his whole life is lived in complete trust in God and Christ. However, if we ask what those words mean when read in the light of the preceding argument rather than in the light of the argument that follows, we find ourselves in difficulty. If I am dead; if I live no longer but Christ lives in me, a statement about the life I live in the flesh would seem to refer to my outward life in contrast to the inner life, which is now the life of Christ. But we have already seen that these words, in the context that follows, can hardly bear this meaning. They refer to the whole life of the Christian.

The first sentence in verse 20 has a different view of the life of a Christian from that expressed in the rest of verse 20 and in verse 21. The ego dies to be replaced by Christ, and the Christian man is substantially changed. In the rest of the verse, on the other hand, the Christian man undergoes not a change in substance but a change in the centre of his trust. The death he went through did not change his nature but changed his allegiance. He still lives in the flesh, expecting death and resurrection with Christ.

45

I conclude that the first sentence of verse 20 is a perfectly understandable gloss on Paul's argument. Paul's mention of death could not but suggest to a theologian living in the Hellenistic world the mystical change of nature whereby an initiate was incorporated into the divine life and deified. Compare the prayer to Hermes, "Come to me Lord Hermes, as babies to women's wombs . . . I know you, Hermes, and you know me. I am you and you are I."[1]

1. British Museum Papyrus cxxii, F. G. Kenyon, *Greek Papyri in the British Museum*, i.116; R. Reitzenstein, *Poimandres* (Leipzig 1904; reprinted Darmstadt 1966), pp. 20f.

3.2, 5 omit ἀκοης; read ἐκ for ἐξ

The expression ἐξ ἀκοῆς πίστεως has proved extraordinarily difficult to explain. Lipsius lists four possible translations: (i) "on the basis of the gift of hearing that faith awakened by the preaching of the crucified one has bestowed"; (ii) "on the basis of the gift of hearing given by the teaching of the Faith"; (iii) "on the basis of the tidings or preaching of faith"; and (iv) "on the basis of the message that is appropriated through faith". Lipsius and Lightfoot adopt the first translation, but Oepke and Schlier have revived the third possibility, which takes ἀκοή to mean "the message" or "preaching". Lipsius succinctly destroys this latter translation by the double argument, "the object of the proclamation is not the πίστις, but the gospel; Paul would then have written ἐκ πίστεως ἀκοῆς". Lipsius's own translation, "on the basis of faith's gift of hearing, *or* listening", provides Paul with a new and rather strange doctrine, that the Spirit is given to Christians because through faith they have acquired a new aptitude to listen. Nothing more is heard of this new sense, but throughout this passage, and in other Pauline contexts, the key factor is faith, and faith alone. This section concludes with the statement, "so those who live by faith (οἱ ἐκ πίστεως) are blessed along with the faithful man Abraham" (3.9). None of Lipsius's possible translations, nor any other that has been suggested, provides a clear sense for a phrase that looks so simple; ἐξ ἀκοῆς πίστεως should provide a natural and easy antithesis to ἐξ ἔργων νόμου, but there proves to be nothing natural and easy about it at all.

I suspect that ἀκοῆς was added as a gloss, both here and in verse 5. A later generation would take πίστις to mean "the Christian Faith", and a glossator might feel the need to make explicit in the margin that, just as the Law demanded works, the Faith demanded hearing. Those who attended to the authoritatively formulated Faith received the Holy Spirit. Paul's meaning was, of course, rather different. Not by doing the works prescribed in the Law did the Galatians receive the Spirit, but by trusting in God who gave Jesus Christ to be crucified for them. "Faith" is contrasted with "works" not with "Law".

Alternatively, one might suppose that the glossator meant by ἀκοή Christian preaching in contrast to the Law ("not from works which the Law demands, but from faith which the preaching asks"), and that his gloss had been incorporated into the text in the wrong position, before πίστεως instead of after it.

3.3 omit the verse

The argument in verses 1 and 2 and in verse 5 is that the Galatians are being bewitched into thinking that they need something in addition to the Spirit they received by faith. The assumption is that God who gave them the Spirit is still bestowing the Spirit in rich profusion. But God is also giving the Spirit to those Christians who are Jews, and Paul has to make clear that the Spirit is given to those who live by faith, whether Jew or Gentile.

Verse 3 is not very clear, but whatever it means it can hardly have belonged originally to this context. The Galatians are upbraided for falling away from their former spiritual way into a fleshly mode of life, with the implication that they should return to the spiritual, whereas the whole point of the argument is that the Galatians should remember that the Spirit they were given and still enjoy was given as they had faith, before they had any thought of submitting to the works of the Law. Verse 3 asks the senseless Galatians to return to being spiritual; the surrounding argument reminds them on what terms they received the Spirit.[1] I think verse 3 was a gloss making clear why morally the Galatians were "foolish" (verse 1). Their senselessness is established by referring to the commonplace antithesis, πνεῦμα–σάρξ.

1. Cf. Bruno Bauer, op. cit., pp. 33f.

3.4 omit the verse

Verse 4 seems to refer forward to verse 5; τοσαῦτα must refer to something, and so far the works of the Spirit have not been explicitly mentioned. For that reason I suspect that verse 4 is a comment on verse 5, and comment which originally stood in the margin. The experiences are good experiences, not experiences of persecution. This gloss is probably the continuation of the previous gloss, and makes the moral point that only senseless people would allow the spiritual experiences they had previously enjoyed by living spiritually to go for nothing—if indeed such experiences could ever be in vain.

3.6 omit καθως Αβρααμ επιστευσεν τω θεω και ελογισθη αυτω εις δικαιοσυνην

In verses 6 to 9 we come to a well-loved theme of Paul, and begin with a citation from Gen. 15.6 which is also used at the beginning of the section about Abraham in Rom. 4. Gal. 3.6, however, does not seem to follow at all well from the preceding verse, and takes on significance only when considered in the larger context that is to follow. Bruno Bauer argued from this sudden introduction of Abraham without any explanation that the author of Galatians was building up the document with well-known phrases from Romans, the significance of which he expected his readers to see immediately. This thesis is not intrinsically likely, but Lipsius's counter-hypothesis, that Paul is alluding to slogans of the Jewish Christian agitators, seems equally unlikely. Against Bruno Bauer, a compiler would not go to the trouble of writing a new work unless he had a slightly new purpose in mind, and then his writing would be likely to be polished and purposeful, not disjointed and hard to follow. To see the work of a compiler such as Bruno Bauer has in mind we have only to turn to the Epistle to the Ephesians, with its stately full-phrased style. But a controversialist such as imagined by Lipsius would be careful to pick out his opponent's misuse of Scripture much more clearly and decisively; it is hard to see just what the agitators could have been saying at this point.

Although Bruno Bauer's hypothesis does not account for the facts, it remains true that Abraham is introduced without warning and without a clear connection either with what goes before or with what comes after. Abraham's relation to God is not so important in this context as the relation of the Gentiles to him.

A further difficulty is that the quotation from Scripture is introduced without ceremony in verse 6, while verse 7 begins προϊδοῦσα δὲ ἡ γραφή, as though Scripture had not already been cited (cf. Rom. 9.15, 17: τῷ Μωϋσεῖ γὰρ λέγει . . . λέγει γὰρ ἡ γραφὴ τῷ Φαραώ. . . . The reading γέγραπται in Gal. 3.6 by F G is to be rejected).

Finally, the appeal to *know* in verse 7 is not dependent on the citation from Gen. 15.6 in verse 6. The fact that Abraham was justified because he believed does not prove that men of faith are sons of Abraham. The ἄρα in verse 7 directs our attention back, and the argument to which we are directed is not the argument in verse 6 but the argument in verses 1–5. The fact that men of faith have patently received the Holy Spirit is grounds for the apostle to say, "Know then that those who live by faith, these are Abraham's sons". There is more arguing to be done before this appeal can be fully secured in the minds of the Galatians, but the obvious blessing which has come to them from God provides the basis and starting-point of the argument to follow in verses 8 to 14, and beyond.

I suggest that, for all these reasons, verse 6 is a gloss.

Why was the gloss ever made? The argument in verses 7–9 proceeds on the assumption that the faith of the Gentiles is the basis on which God justifies them; that, in fact, is stated in verse 7: "God justifies the Gentiles for faith". The context shows that Paul believes this because of what he has seen happen before his eyes in Galatia (verses 1–5), but a glossator might well feel that Paul's proof text to show the connection between faith and justification could also be quoted in the context of an argument where Scripture is obviously important. This perfectly reasonable gloss was then, I conjecture, copied in to the text at what seemed, to a later scribe, to be the appropriate place.

3.15 omit ομως ανθρωπου κεκυρωμενην διαθηκην ουδεις αθετει η επιδιατασσεται

The opening of verse 15 means that Paul is about to argue to God from human customs. The sentence beginning ὅμως (ὁμῶς)

49

(which probably means "likewise"; Bauer-A.-G.; Jeremias, *ZNW* 52 (1961), pp. 127f; R. Keydell, *ZNW* 54 (1963), pp. 145f) states that, according to human practice, no one sets aside a will, or adds a codicil to it. The attempt to argue that the two words ἀνθρώπου and οὐδείς belong together, so that "no one" includes the testator as well, is forced; οὐδείς implies that someone other than the testator would want to set aside the will or to modify it. If the will is one made under Mattanah procedure, that is, coming into force straightaway, during the testator's lifetime (E. Bammel, *NTS* 6 (1960), pp. 313–19), this comment is perfectly correct, but the surrounding context concerns the testator alone. Paul wants to argue that God, having made a covenant or will benefiting Abraham and his seed, has not changed it when he gives the Law. Verse 15b, on the other hand, introduces the possibility that the second will is an attempt to set aside or modify the original will by someone other than the testator, and implies that the introduction of the Law was the setting aside of the promise, or the adding of a falsifying codicil. The whole set of ideas would be impossible in Paul's thought, and I suggest that verse 15b was originally a gloss. The Law for Paul remains God's gift. The gloss contains ideas which did not become current in the Church until the time of the Epistle of Barnabas. Furthermore, it is a comment made in the light of what yet has to be stated in verses 17 and 18. The introductory word ὅμως invariably introduces a comparison with something said earlier (Ps. Clem. *Hom.* 3.15.3; 19.23.1; *The Adventures of Saint Macarius of Rome*, ed. Vassiliev, in *Anecdota Graeco-Byzantina* i (Moscow 1893), p. 137), and this is one more indication that the sentence is a gloss to verses 17 and 18, and not an original part of the text, for nothing has yet been said with which a comparison can be made.

3.16 omit δε
    omit ου λεγει· και τοις σπερμασιν, ως επι πολλων, αλλ ως εφ
    ενος· και τω σπερματι σου, ος εστιν Χριστος

The δέ is omitted in verse 16 by D* F G it vg, and was possibly inserted in an attempt to make a connection with the gloss in verse 15.

In the first half of the verse καὶ τῷ σπέρματι αὐτοῦ must refer to Abraham's descendants. Not only is σπέρμα usually a collective noun (Rom. 4.13, 16, 18; 9.7f; Gal. 3.29), but the context, verses 17 and 18, is talking about those descendants of Abraham to whom the Law was given. Verse 16b is therefore a gloss that takes σπέρμα to refer to a single descendant, and identifies that descendant with Christ. It is very hard to imagine Paul's saying that Christ was the one who received the promises promised to Abraham; Jesus Christ is rather the means by which the blessing promised to Abraham goes out to the Gentiles, so that those who have faith, both Jews and Gentiles, might receive the Spirit (3.1–14).

The existence of the gloss is recognized by Weisse, Cramer, Burton, and many others.

When the glosses in verses 15 and 16 are put to one side, we are left with a relatively straightforward human analogy for God's dealings with men. In this analogy διαθήκη means "covenant" and probably not "will". (Even Mattanah procedure does not solve all the problems of the will analogy, because under that procedure the gift becomes the possession of the legatee straightaway. The Gentiles had had to wait.) Just as no man who entered into a covenant in which he promised to give certain gifts would later fall from his promise just because it was necessary also to make some new arrangement with the party to the covenant, so God would not fall from his promise to Abraham just because later the Law was introduced. The Law is also an arrangement of God's with men (that is clearly implied in verse 18), but it cannot be his means of giving the inheritance, because the inheritance was firmly promised, and what is promised cannot be turned into something conditional that has to be worked for. "God showed himself gracious to Abraham by making a promise."

Paul's theology is a theology of God's unfailing promise to men.

3.19, 20 omit διαταγεις δι αγγελων εν χειρι μεσιτου. ο δε μεσιτης ενος ουκ εστιν, ο δε θεος εις εστιν

The construction of the second sentence in verse 19 is difficult. The participle διαταγείς does not agree with the subject of the immediately preceding verb ἐπήγγελται, nor with the subject of ἔλθῃ, τὸ σπέρμα, but with the subject of προσετέθη, ὁ νόμος understood. This participle introduces an entirely new thought into the context. The passive verb προσετέθη implies that the Law was added by God, and the point at issue is, Why did God add the Law to his other dealings with Israel? The thought introduced by διαταγείς is in answer to the question, What does the method by which the Law was given tell us about its status? The answer to this question is probably that the employment of a middle-man, Moses, shows that the multitude of angels were the other party to the transaction, not God, who would need no middle-man (Klöpper, Steck (p. 61), Lietzmann, A. Schweitzer, Loisy, Duncan, Oepke). That answer contradicts the implication behind προσετέθη. But even if the answer to the question could be brought into closer harmony with verse 19a by supposing that the employment of a middle-man indicates that the Law is a contract between two parties, whereas God alone is responsible for the fulfilment of his promise (Lightfoot, &c.), the question itself remains a foreign body in the context. With Baljon and Völter I regard verses 19b and 20 as a gloss.[1]

The purpose of the gloss was to show that the Law had been given by the angels and not by God. The gloss represents ideas that came to their fruition in heretical Gnosticism, as Schlier shows conclusively, without drawing the inference that this is a gloss.[2]

The gloss is not *completely* foreign to the sentence it is glossing. In that sentence the question, "What then is the Law?" receives a positive answer, to be sure, but an answer that would be very difficult for a Jew to accept. The answer is most probably that the Law was introduced to check transgressions. The other possibility, that the Law was given to multiply transgressions (Rom. 4.15; 5.20), would require a great deal more explaining before the reader could see that this would be a positive function—and the form of the question and answer demands that a positive function be in mind.

The question now arises, Could Paul the Jew have possibly proposed this function for the Law? I think one could argue that Paul sets a very high value on this function. In 2.15, at the beginning of his answer to Cephas, he assumes quite simply, without any trace of irony, that the Gentiles are sinners and the Jews are not. He does not mean that the Jews are by nature wholly righteous, but he probably means that the Jews have been preserved from the corruption prevalent in the Gentile world. They have been protected by God's giving them the Law.

1. Cramer omits everything of these two verses after τί οὖν;

2. Op. cit., pp. 157f. See especially Cerinthus (Epiph., *adv. haer.* 28.1.3; 2.1), Simon Magus (Iren., *adv. haer.* i.23.3), Saturninus (*Iren.*, i.24.2), and Basilides (*Iren.*, i.24.5).

3.22 omit Ιησου Χριστου

The fulfilment of the promise to Abraham about the blessings in store for the Gentiles came about when the Gentiles were able to trust in Jesus Christ (3.14), but the promise itself, when made, contained no mention of the Messiah, let alone Jesus Christ. The fact that a promise was made, however, implied that the only attitude men could take to the promise was to trust him who made the promise. The making of a promise by God meant that he is gracious and to be trusted (3.18).

If this general line of argument is a faithful reflection of Paul's case, I suspect that Paul did not write ἡ ἐπαγγελία ἐκ πίστεως Ἰησοῦ Χριστοῦ. The promise itself simply required faith, and was to be given to those who believed; the specific content of the faith had yet to be revealed. Of course, when Jesus Christ came, faith received its ultimate object and the promise was fulfilled, but Paul's argument held even before the final revelation had been made. I therefore regard Ἰησοῦ Χριστοῦ as an understandable but incorrect gloss. The words are omitted in the Ethiopic version.

3.23–5 omit the three verses

Verses 23–5 speak in the first person plural. Who, then, are "we"? "We" must either be "we Jews", in which case the Gentiles are excluded, as not having had the Law, or "we" must be "we men", in which case Jews and Gentiles are both conceived as having their own "law" which confines them until faith comes. The first possibility fits the immediate context better, which has been concerned with the Law given to Israel years after the covenant with Moses. On the other hand, the idea that the law is like a custodian or guide of the young is drawn from popular Greek philosophy (Plutarch, *Table Talk*, Bk. iii proem, *Mor.* 645B, C; Pseudo Epictetus, Schweighäuser Frag. 97), and the sentiments expressed fit in well with a universal picture of morality and beyond.

What enables men to pass out of the care of the "pedagogue" is the coming of faith. On Paul's previous argument this expression, the coming of faith, raises difficulties. Abraham himself was already faithful (3.9), so that faith was already there. Indeed, faith can hardly be understood, in the context of the previous argument, as an entity that *comes* at all. Faith is trust, not a given thing. It begins to appear that faith in verses 23–5 means the principle of faith, or even "the Christian Faith" rather than trust. If that is so, the argument must be a universal argument. It belongs wholly in an atmosphere in which Christianity is aspiring to be the universal religion, and in which Old Testament Law is just one manifestation of law which binds all men. The problem about why God added his gift of the Law to his earlier covenant of promise has fallen away into the background, to be replaced by a more general moral problem about external restraint and free self-governing life in the faith. Paul is talking about the coming of the seed to whom the promise was made (verse 19); verses 21–3 talk about the coming of faith. Paul is dealing with history, while verses 21–3 are dealing with the moral progress of men.

These verses are a profound commentary on Paul, but commentary. They presuppose a different problem, and use a technical vocabulary in a different sense.

3.26 omit θεου; omit της; omit εν Χριστω Ιησου

Verse 26 begins a new section in the second person. The chief idea in the verse is somewhat surprising. Chapter 4 is to contain a great deal about "sons of God", but hitherto the argument has turned on whether or not the Gentile Christians are sons of Abraham. The term "sons of Abraham" occurs in 3.7 in a prominent position, and the theme governs the argument down to verse 22. Furthermore, the theme recurs below in verse 29, where "Abraham's" or "Abraham's seed" implies "sons of Abraham".

There is a strong case for asking whether our printed text represents what Paul wrote, and whether Paul's original letter has not been glossed.

The textual evidence strongly suggests that glossators have been at work. Marcion, according to Tertullian, read "omnes enim filii estis fidei", a reading also found in Hilary (*Hom. in Ps.* 91). Clement of Alexandria gives πάντες γὰρ υἱοί ἐστε διὰ πίστεως θεοῦ ἐν Χριστῷ 'Ιησοῦ; p[46] reads πάντες γὰρ υἱοὶ θεοῦ (ἐστε) διὰ πίστεως

54

$Χριστοῦ$ '$Ιησοῦ$; and P follows our printed texts to $ἐστε$, but then reads $διὰ$ $πίστεως$ and no more.

I can see no reason why either $θεοῦ$ or $ἐν$ $Χριστῷ$ '$Ιησοῦ$ would be omitted by Marcion or the other witnesses, but every reason why they would, almost inevitably, have been added to an original text which read $πάντες$ $γὰρ$ $υἱοί$ $ἐστε$ $διὰ$ $πίστεως$.

The sonship thus referred to would originally have been sonship of Abraham.

3.28 omit the verse

Verse 26, in the shorter form which I have conjectured was the original, is now properly supplemented by another striking image to show how the faith of the Gentiles in Christ leads them to become Abraham's children also.

Baptism is the mark of a decisive change of allegiance which binds a man to Christ (1 Cor. 1.13); baptism is the sign of faith. Verse 29 then naturally takes up both verse 27 and the key idea in verse 26, that the Galatians are sons of Abraham by faith.

Verse 28 begins to look out of place. The intermediate verse argues that baptism into Christ obliterates the old distinctions of Jew and Gentile, slave and free, male and female, and creates a new unity in him. That view is the logical end of Paul's position, but here he is arguing that the Gentiles have attained the full status of Abraham's sons by faith. He is not concerned, at this point in his argument, to say that Jewishness no longer matters (much less concerned with slavery or the differences between the sexes); he has the more urgent task on his hands of assuring the Gentile Christians that they are already Abraham's seed by faith, and do not need to be circumcised.

Verse 28 expresses a view of the Church that grew up after Paul's day, when Jewish Christians were forced to leave Judaism just as decisively as Gentile Christians had to leave paganism. Paul was living in a different time, when the Jews who believed that Jesus was Messiah still had hopes of convincing their fellow-Jews, and when Gentile Christians either became proselytes or joined the Gentile congregations Paul was founding alongside the believing synagogues.

3.29 omit σπερμα

The word σπέρμα is omitted by 1845* (according to von Soden); B reads σπέρματος, and 404 547 read τέκνα. The glosses are correct in sense, but the diversity of readings suggests that Paul originally wrote simply, "If you are Christ's, then you are Abraham's, heirs according to the promise."

The discussion begun at the beginning of chapter 3, more explicitly in verse 7, is brought to a triumphant conclusion. The Galatians cannot possibly do anything more to become sons of Abraham, for they are sons of Abraham already.

4.1–10 omit 1–3; 8–10
(omit 4, 5?)
6 omit του υιου; read υμων for ημων

The images employed in verses 1–3, on the one hand, and verses 4–7, on the other hand, are strictly incompatible. In verses 1–3 the heir is held in subjection while he is a minor and is little different from a slave although lord of all. On the appointed day he becomes free. In verses 4–7 a slave is ransomed and adopted as a son. He is really a slave, not as good as a slave, because verse 7 explicitly states that only after adoption does he become heir. In verses 1–3 the enslaved man was always heir, despite his bondage.

If verses 1–3 and verses 4–7 are different, the next section, verses 8–10, belongs with the former rather than the latter. In verse 3, where an exposition of the parable about the heir who is a minor is given, particular attention is focused on the guardians who were appointed to look after him. In the interpretation these guardians are identified with τὰ στοιχεῖα τοῦ κόσμου. Verses 8–10 continue with the same emphasis on these governing powers, and argue the senselessness of returning to childhood subjection after having come to know God. Verses 4–7, on the other hand, contain no reference to slave-owners or anything of the sort.

If verses 1–3 and 8–10 form a single distinct argument, it is clear that Paul could not have been responsible, because the dangers these verses are designed to avert are not the dangers that confronted the Galatians. These dangers are specifically described in verse 10 as keeping days, and months, and seasons, and years, and the observances here listed are linked with subjection to the "elemental powers of the world". It seems that the astronomical times were connected, in this system, with heavenly powers.

Bruno Bauer has already raised the question whether or not Paul could have described Judaism in this way, putting Judaism on a level with pagan superstitions.[1] I should add that Paul could not have described the Law in such a derogatory way so soon after he had stated that the Law was given by God (3.19). Paul could hardly have described Judaism like this, particularly as he acknowledged the right of the Jewish Christian congregations to go on existing as part of Judaism.

A second reason for doubting that Paul wrote this to the Galatians is the terms in which the new way is described. Orthodox Judaism is scarcely distinguished by its attention to the calendar, and commentators who have argued that the list in verse 10 is an apt description of such Judaism have found difficulty in saying what the ἐνιαυτούς refer to.[2] And no orthodox Jew would observe days, months, and seasons to placate the στοιχεῖα. Certainly there were corners of Judaism that showed a particular interest in the calendar and in the course of the sun and the moon and the stars; the Book of the Heavenly Luminaries (Ethiopian Enoch, 72–82), the Book of Jubilees, and the Qumran Writings all describe the laws of the heavenly movements according to which men should live their lives.[3] But the heavenly bodies are under the control of God. According to the view under scrutiny and attack in verses 8–10, however, the heavenly bodies are controlled by στοιχεῖα, powers subordinate to God and to some extent independent of his control. This sort of position is not Judaism but Jewish Gnosticism or, more probably, Jewish Christian Gnosticism. The best parallel I know is in the heresy of the Elchesaites, described by Hippolytus in *Philosophumena* ix. 13–17.[4] The Elchesaites preached conformity with the Law, including circumcision, a reincarnational Christology, baptism, and the use of incantations. They were very interested in astrology and mathematics, and counselled their followers not to begin new works or baptize on certain days for "there are evil stars of impiety".[5] They advocated a system that could well be described as a falling back into paganism, for all its appeal to the Law; the key feature is that it ascribed a continuing malignant power over men to the heavenly bodies and the angels behind them. (Much the same sort of system is being attacked in the pseudonymous Epistle to the Colossians.)

57

Finally, it has always been puzzling why Paul should have omitted the main tenets of Judaism in this, his first specific list of what the Galatians were being asked to observe. Even if observing days, months, seasons, and years could be taken to describe the practices of Judaism, it is puzzling that circumcision and the food laws were omitted. But if this section is a later addition to Paul's original letter, we can well understand that the later theologian would pick out only those features of the heresy that he wished to attack; he felt free to insert such an attack into Galatians because, in its main respects, the heresy coincided with the Judaism to which the original recipients of Paul's letter were in danger of succumbing.

That verses 1–3, 8–10 have now been added to verses 4–7 is shown by the way verse 3 is dependent on verse 4. They are obviously linked: "when we were minors we were enslaved . . . but when the fulness of time came . . ." But, apart from the previously noted difference between the two images, there is a further misunderstanding of verses 4–5 in verse 3. Verse 3 is talking about pagans, while verses 4–5 are talking about Jews. Jews alone needed to be ransomed from under the Law, for νόμος in this context almost certainly refers to the Mosaic Law and not to law in general (Lipsius against Lightfoot). All references to νόμος in chapter 3 (bar 3.23–5) are explicitly Mosaic, and it is hard to imagine Paul's changing over to a more general consideration of law without notice, in a context where his chief interest is to persuade the Galatians not to adopt the Law of Moses.

If verses 4–5 refer to Jews, we might wonder whether these verses too were not foreign to Paul's argument, particularly because it says, "that *we* should receive adoption".

The answer seems to be that verses 4–5 were not originally written by Paul, but are cited from Jewish Christian liturgy.

The form of verses 4 and 5 marks them off completely from the context. J. B. Lightfoot noted that "the two clauses (in verse 5) correspond to those of the foregoing verse in an inverted order by the grammatical figure called chiasm; 'The Son of God was born a man, that in Him all men might become sons of God; He was born subject to law, that those subject to law might be rescued from bondage.'" That is true, but the introductory part of verse 4 also belongs to the poetic structure; the ὅτε-clause is the first colon, and the main clause the second colon of a six-colon stanza. The colons each have their own verb, and consist of 12,

58

13, 8, 8, 12, 13 syllables respectively; this striking regularity is not to be found in the surrounding verses.

I conclude that verses 4 and 5 originally comprised a short credal affirmation in poetic form. It is possible that Paul himself quoted a Jewish Christian hymn to illustrate his point that the coming of God's Son meant adoption as God's sons for men, but I hesitate to believe that Paul was responsible, because I should have expected Paul to make some reference to the fact that what applied to Jews, who were under the Law, applied also to Gentiles, who were not. The great difficulty in the way of regarding verses 4 and 5 as another gloss is that then the whole section will have been glossed heavily by two different hands, one responsible for verses 1–3, 8–10, and the other responsible for verses 4f. Nevertheless, that seems to be the right solution; and verses 4f would have been the first addition, which helped prompt verses 1–3, 8–10, the second addition.

Paul's argument will then have been as follows. In chapter 3, he has established that there must come a time when God's promises to Abraham would be fulfilled, and the giving of the Law could not change the conditions under which the original promise was made. The promise was made to those who, like Abraham, had faith. The blessing was for Gentiles as well as for Jews. If Gentiles became Christ's by baptism, they obviously also became Abraham's, and heirs according to the promise. Because they are sons of Abraham, God has sent his Spirit to show that they are also sons of God, for that was the promise made to Abraham and his seed. Therefore, as heirs of God's promises made to Abraham, they have no need of any further benefit which circumcision and adherence to the Law were supposed to bring.

In verse 6 p⁴⁶ (Marcion?) Augustine omit τοῦ υἱοῦ, and perhaps we should accept this omission as original, the addition having been made under the influence of verse 4. Also in verse 6 there is another variant we should note. The manuscripts p⁴⁶ ℵ A B C D* F G P etc. read εἰς τὰς καρδίας ἡμῶν. The variant ὑμῶν is supported by K L Ψ 33 81 1836 vg syr (bo), and this variant may well be the original text, altered by some scribes under the influence of ἀπολάβωμεν in verse 5 and of the pious thought that the apostle could not have meant to restrict the operation of the Spirit in any way. There are other strange various readings in this verse and the next, which I cannot understand, but they do not seem to affect the argument in any important respect.

1. Op. cit., p. 50.
2. See a survey of interpretations in Schlier, p. 206, n. 1.
3. See Schlier's excellent collection of citations and his discussion, pp. 204–7.
4. The key passage is cited in Greek by Schlier, p. 206.
5. *Philos.* ix.16.

4.11–20 (*14* omit ὡς Χριστον Ιησουν?)
   omit *17*
   19 omit μεχρις ου μορφωθη Χριστος εν υμιν

The section in which Paul appeals to the Galatians' former personal loyalty raises a number of difficulties. But they are difficulties that arise from our uncertainty about the precise meaning of words or events (οὐδέν με ἠδικήσατε, verse 12; τὸν πειρασμόν, verse 14; τὸ πρότερον, verse 13; ὁ μακαρισμὸς ὑμῶν and the plucking out of eyes, verse 15) and not difficulties that would be resolved by assuming that a Paulinist was drawing on other epistles in order to give colour to his pseudonymous writing. Here the personal details are essential to Paul's appeal, and a little obscure to us.

Bruno Bauer argues that the appeal to become like Paul in verse 12 is so vague in content that it must be due to a Paulinist who wanted to hold the apostle up as an ideal, without being entirely clear as to what it was about him that should be followed. However, the general content of the epistle as a whole makes it clear enough that when Paul says "Become like me" he means that they should rely completely on God who promised to bless Abraham and his seed, and that when he says "as I too [became] like you" he means that he, a Jew, joined them in their Gentile existence, outside the strict observance of all the Law's requirements.

The last words of verse 14, ὡς Χριστὸν 'Ιησοῦν, are certainly surprising, and must refer to Paul's own estimate of the honour they did him. Perhaps we should follow Weisse and ascribe them to a glossator.

The reference in verse 15 to the Galatians' willingness to give Paul their eyes is not a "chilling exaggeration" which no one bound by personal ties to his readers would make (Bruno Bauer), but most probably a reference to the effect on Paul's sight of his illness. The Galatians would have deprived themselves of sight if they could thereby have helped Paul (Bousset, Schlier).

Verse 16 implies that since Paul last saw the Galatians they have come to regard him as an enemy. The high regard the Galatians had for him when he was there has not survived during his absence, and he both appeals to them to follow what is good even though he is not there to remind them of it (verse 18), and wishes to make another visit so that he could be sure of their position and be able to desist from his theological attacks.

In general these verses are clear enough, but two details are very difficult. Pierson and Nagel[1] describe verses 17 and 18 as full of solecisms. However, the end of verse 18 fits well into the context of the general argument, and follows logically from the first part of the verse which, out of context, could be regarded as little more than a platitude. The difficulty, therefore, resides in verse 17 alone. The zeal in verse 18 is zeal ἐν καλῷ, but the zeal in verse 17 is the courting of men's favour, which is οὐ καλῶς. Verse 17 unexpectedly introduces a new factor into the situation between Paul and the Galatians, the activity of certain unnamed men who have both courted the Galatians and threatened them with exclusion from the universal Church, in order to get the Galatians to be deeply concerned about them. The language looks like a comment on verse 18 rather than an introduction to verse 18, for Paul does not go on specifically to wish that he might refute these ecclesiastical statesmen or that the Galatians might reject them, but rather to wish that the Galatians might return to the truth by recollecting what they had once accepted from him and could accept from him again. For these reasons I think that verse 17 was a gloss that reflected a situation when an increasingly confident Jewish Christian church was sending envoys to the Gentile Christian churches, threatening them with exclusion from the Church if they did not own the envoys' authority. It may have been true in Paul's day that travelling theologians were advocating the circumcision of Gentile Christians, but I doubt if excommunication from the universal Church was yet one of the threats in their armoury. But, be that as it may, the issue in this section lies between Paul and the Galatians, and there is no room for third parties.

The second difficulty is caused by the clause at the end of verse 19, μέχρις οὗ μορφωθῇ Χριστὸς ἐν ὑμῖν. Presumably the apostle compares himself to a mother who by labour produces a new child, a corporate Christ, which has been formed in her womb. Apart from the difficult telescoping of the idea of formation in the womb and the idea of birth-pangs, the whole image fails, because formation in the womb cannot follow birth-pangs.[2]

The verb ὠδίνω has a well-established figurative sense, to be in throes and agonies of thought, and in this sense runs parallel to the word ἀποροῦμαι in verse 20, to be in mental perplexity. I conjecture that the last clause of verse 19 is the work of a glossator who took a figurative word literally, and made it the occasion for a spiritual metaphor. When the gloss is put to one side, I should regard verse 19a as the conclusion to the preceding sentence, and verse 20 as a new sentence. The gloss was perhaps originally designed to attach to ἄρτι: "I wish I could be with you, now, until Christ be formed in you."

1. Op. cit., p. 64, n. 1.
2. Cf. Pierson and Naber, op. cit., p. 46, n. 1: "nec magis sensum assequimur vs. 19, nam non partu foetus formatur, sed quamdiu in utero gestatur. Quid est illud πάλιν?"

4.21–31 omit *4.24b* (αὐται γαρ . . .)*–27*
         omit *4.30*

Paul begins a new argument against these Gentile Christians who thought they should become Jews, with a renewed appeal to the Scriptures. If they want to submit to the Mosaic Law, they would first have to listen to the whole Law, the Bible.

He then argues from the case of Abraham's two sons that Scripture makes a distinction between merely physical descent from Abraham, and descent that results from God's fulfilment of his promise. Up to verse 23 the argument is about the two sons and the presence and absence of God's specific promise at their conception. The argument could apply to Jewish Christians as well as to Gentile Christians, because it implies that the true sons of Abraham are those who live by faith in the fulfilment of God's promises, whether they be Jews or Gentiles. Jewish Christians might still observe the full regulations of the Law, so long as they did not rely on them for their justification, or hold that Gentiles needed to become Jews in order to be justified by God.

Verses 24b–27, on the other hand, are concerned with the

allegorical significance of the two mothers. Hagar is taken to mean Mount Sinai, the earthly Jerusalem and Judaism, while Sarah is taken to mean the heavenly Jerusalem and the Church, Mother of the faithful. The allegory implies that men had to choose between belonging to Judaism and belonging to the Church, and this sort of choice was not yet necessary in Paul's day. The identification of an enslaved people with the present Jerusalem possibly referred to, and followed from, the historical subordination of the Jews to the Romans (Pelagius).

Verse 28 returns to the original scriptural argument. This verse, too, is in the second person plural, like 21–3, not the first person plural of verses 24–7. Verse 28 brings the argument back from the mothers to the sons, and it does not depend on the external fact of the difference of status between a slave-woman and a free woman, but on the different circumstances accompanying the birth of the two sons. Isaac was born as a result of God's promise to Abraham. We have already seen that Paul's key argument about Abraham is that he is the recipient of God's promises, so that 4.21–3 and this verse fit in very well with previous material belonging to the earliest stratum of the epistle.

The section from 4.29 to 5.1 draws on Jewish traditions about the enmity of Ishmael for Isaac in order to explain that Jewish hostility to those who believed in Christ was to be expected, and was by no means an argument for abandoning the freedom that was the heritage of the children of promise after the type of Isaac, Jews and Gentiles. Paul never underestimated the seriousness of Jewish opposition to the Jews and Gentiles who believed in Christ. The issue was deadly serious, but the whole force of his position would have been weakened had he adopted the position represented in 4.24b–27. He was not arguing for membership of a spiritual Jerusalem over against membership of an earthly Jerusalem, but arguing that the earthly Jerusalem, the centre of homage for Gentile Christians as well as Jewish, should be true to Abraham's faith.

Although Paul reckoned with Jewish opposition to the gospel, opposition in which he had been involved, it is very unlikely that he would want the Church to turn on Jews who did not believe. Verse 30, which assumes that the Church is organized as a separate entity, with power to harry unbelieving Jews, seems hardly to belong to Paul's day, and looks like a later gloss. When the gloss is removed, the consequential διό, at the beginning of verse 31, follows much better from the preceding argument. It was hard to see how the fact that we were children of the free woman and not of the slave followed from an injunction to cast out the slave and her son. When verse 30 is set aside, our being children of the free woman follows from our being persecuted by unbelieving Jews. If 4. 21–24a, 28, 29, 31 cannot be isolated, all 4. 21–31 is not Paul.

5.11 omit the first ἔτι

The evidence for the omission of the first ἔτι is as follows: D* F^{gr} G 1739 d g go arm Victorin Ambrst Hier Pelag. The text with ἔτι can hardly be right, since it implies that once, since becoming an apostle, he preached circumcision (*pace* Meyer, Lipsius, Schlier); his argument would in that case be, If I were still preaching circumcision as I once did, why has the persecution still continued? An admission that he had ever preached circumcision to Gentiles would entirely destroy the case he presented in the early chapters of the epistle.

Nevertheless, the rhetorical question implies that he has been accused of preaching circumcision.[1] The circumcision of Timothy, reported in Acts 16.1–3, might have suggested to ignorant or ill-informed observers that Paul used to preach that Gentiles should be circumcised. It follows that Galatians 5.11, without the first ἔτι, is a possible sentence implying real circumstances, and there is no need to follow Weisse and strike out the whole verse.

Before we can be sure that the first ἔτι was originally a gloss, we have to see whether a glossator would have had a plausible reason for adding his comment. Zahn,[2] the only commentator to my knowledge who accepts this shorter text, suggests that ἔτι was added on the model of 1.10. I should add that the same ignorance about the true meaning of Timothy's circumcision, which led to the charge Paul was rebutting, could also have led a glossator to attempt to take account of what he believed to be the case, that Paul in his apostolic time had once circumcised a Gentile.

---

1. This conclusion is perhaps supported by the denial of the same charge in verse 8: "This pressure is not from him who called you" (that is, not from Paul). All commentators, however, take the calling to be from God, and I am not sure enough of my ground to put much weight on this passage. John Locke and Henry Owen are the only exceptions to the ruling opinion among commentators that I can discover. John Locke, op. cit., p. 35: "This Expression, of *him that called* or *calleth* you, he used before, Ch. *I.* 6. and in both Places means himself." See note on 1.6 above.
2. *Der Brief des Paulus an die Galater* (2nd edn, Leipzig 1907), pp. 255–6, n. 79.

13 ὑμεῖς γὰρ ἐπ᾽ ἐλευθερίᾳ ἐκλήθητε, ἀδελφοί·
   μόνον μὴ τὴν ἐλευθερίαν εἰς ἀφορμὴν τῇ σαρκί,
   ἀλλὰ διὰ τῆς ἀγάπης δουλεύετε ἀλλήλοις.
14 ὁ γὰρ πᾶς νόμος ἐν ἑνὶ λόγῳ πεπλήρωται,
   ἐν τῷ· ἀγαπήσεις τὸν πλησίον σου ὡς σεαυτόν.
15 εἰ δὲ ἀλλήλους δάκνετε καὶ κατεσθίετε,
   βλέπετε μὴ ὑπ᾽ ἀλλήλων ἀναλωθῆτε.

16 λέγω δέ, πνεύματι περιπατεῖτε
   καὶ ἐπιθυμίαν σαρκὸς οὐ μὴ τελέσητε.
17 ἡ γὰρ σὰρξ ἐπιθυμεῖ κατὰ τοῦ πνεύματος,
   τὸ δὲ πνεῦμα κατὰ τῆς σαρκός,
   ταῦτα γὰρ ἀλλήλοις ἀντίκειται,
   ἵνα μὴ ἃ ἐὰν θέλητε ταῦτα ποιῆτε.

18 εἰ δὲ πνεύματι ἄγεσθε,
   οὐκ ἐστὲ ὑπὸ νόμον.

19 φανερὰ δέ ἐστιν τὰ ἔργα τῆς σαρκός,
   ἅτινά ἐστιν πορνεία, ἀκαθαρσία, ἀσέλγεια,
20 εἰδωλολατρία, φαρμακεία,
   ἔχθραι, ἔρις, ζῆλος, θυμοί, ἐριθεῖαι,
21 διχοστασίαι, αἱρέσεις, φθόνοι,
   μέθαι, κῶμοι, καὶ τὰ ὅμοια τούτοις,
   ἃ προλέγω ὑμῖν καθὼς προεῖπον,
   ὅτι οἱ τὰ τοιαῦτα πράσσοντες
   βασιλείαν θεοῦ οὐ κληρονομήσουσιν.

22 ὁ δὲ καρπὸς τοῦ πνεύματός ἐστιν
   ἀγάπη, χαρά, εἰρήνη,
   μακροθυμία, χρηστότης, ἀγαθωσύνη,
23 πίστις, πραΰτης, ἐγκράτεια·
   κατὰ τῶν τοιούτων οὐκ ἔστιν νόμος.

24 οἱ δὲ τοῦ Χριστοῦ Ἰησοῦ
   τὴν σάρκα ἐσταύρωσαν
   σὺν τοῖς παθήμασιν
   καὶ ταῖς ἐπιθυμίαις.

65

25 εἰ ζῶμεν πνεύματι,
πνεύματι καὶ στοιχῶμεν.

26 μὴ γινώμεθα κενόδοξοι·
ἀλλήλους προκαλούμενοι,
ἀλλήλοις φθονοῦντες.

6.1 ἀδελφοί, ἐὰν καὶ προλημφθῇ ἄνθρωπος ἐν τινι παραπτώματι, ὑμεῖς
οἱ πνευματικοὶ καταρτίζετε τὸν τοιοῦτον ἐν πνεύματι πραΰτητος,
σκοπῶν σεαυτόν, μὴ καὶ σὺ πειρασθῇς.

2 ἀλλήλων τὰ βάρη βαστάζετε, καὶ οὕτως ἀναπληρώσετε τὸν νόμον
τοῦ Χριστοῦ.

3 εἰ γὰρ δοκεῖ τις εἶναί τι μηδὲν ὤν, φρεναπατᾷ ἑαυτόν.

4 τὸ δὲ ἔργον ἑαυτοῦ δοκιμαζέτω ἕκαστος, καὶ τότε εἰς ἑαυτὸν
5 μόνον τὸ καύχημα ἕξει, καὶ οὐκ εἰς ἕτερον. ἕκαστος γὰρ τὸ ἴδιον
φορτίον βαστάσει.

6 κοινωνείτω δὲ ὁ κατηχούμενος τὸν λόγον τῷ κατηχοῦντι ἐν πᾶσιν
ἀγαθοῖς.

7 μὴ πλανᾶσθε·
θεὸς οὐ μυκτηρίζεται.
ὃ γὰρ ἐὰν σπείρῃ ἄνθρωπος,
τοῦτο καὶ θερίσει·
8 ὅτι ὁ σπείρων εἰς τὴν σάρκα ἑαυτοῦ
ἐκ τῆς σαρκὸς θερίσει φθοράν·
ὁ δὲ σπείρων εἰς τὸ πνεῦμα
ἐκ τοῦ πνεύματος θερίσει ζωὴν αἰώνιον.

9 τὸ δὲ καλὸν ποιοῦντες μὴ ἐγκακῶμεν· καιρῷ γὰρ ἰδίῳ θερίσομεν
10 μὴ ἐκλυόμενοι. ἄρα οὖν ὡς καιρὸν ἔχομεν, ἐργαζώμεθα τὸ ἀγαθὸν
πρὸς πάντας, μάλιστα δὲ πρὸς τοὺς οἰκείους τῆς πίστεως.

If Paul wanted to warn the Galatians against Judaizers who were
trying to persuade them to be circumcised, it seems strange that
he should suddenly also warn them against antinomianism. This
change of emphasis has prompted a number of interesting
theories, the most famous of which is Lütgert's.

Wilhelm Lütgert,[1] followed by the American scholar J. H. Ropes,[2] has tried to reconcile the attack on antinomianism in this section with the rest of the book by supposing that Paul was fighting on two fronts: against opponents who accused him of betraying the freedom he once preached, of being still a half Jew, as well as against Judaizers who wanted Gentile Christians to be circumcised. The first group of opponents were "Pneumatikoi" who encouraged the Galatians to fall back into pagan ways, and the (rather gentler) passages of polemic against licentiousness and in favour of obedience were directed against them.

The difficulty with this theory is that there is no discernible trace in Galatians that Paul is fighting on two fronts.[3] Yet the problem remains. How can we fit the sort of polemic in this section into the historical situation where Paul is facing a specific attack?

Schmithals[4] has attempted to meet the problem by supposing that the opponents were gnostic Jewish Christians, in effect combining the two groups proposed by Lütgert. The best evidence for Schmithals's theory is to be found in 4.8–10, where Paul seems to be attacking a gnostic position, but I have already tried to show that this attack was not written by Paul, and did not fit his actual opponents. The support his theory seems to find here, in 5.13 to 6.10,[5] I should meet in the same way. But here there are in fact no particular opponents in mind at all, as there were in 4.8–10. This section is directed to all Christians, to meet the common human temptations. It has nothing in particular to do with the urgent problem Paul was trying to meet in his original letter.

Far from being a sustained argument, 5.13–6.10 is really a collection of moral admonitions telling Christians at large what are their duties. There is no connection between one admonition and the next, except sometimes a similarity of subject or a catchphrase; the collector is not pursuing a connected argument. The collection is similar to the collection called *The Two Ways* (Didache 1–6; Barnabas 18–21), and to the Epistle of James and parts of the Synoptic Gospels. I think that there are fifteen separate pieces of advice, each stylistically distinct, and distinct in thought, from its neighbour. Once this formal characteristic is established, it becomes almost impossible to hold that Paul was directly responsible. In order to show clearly the formal characteristics, I have reproduced the whole of the passage in Greek on pp. 65–6 above.

The first saying consists of 5.13-15, seven lines of even length devoted to the warning that if freedom degenerates into individualistic licence, the community can easily destroy itself. The issue is the general issue confronting the Church at all times, but has nothing in particular to do with the Galatians. Their temptation was not to use their freedom as an occasion for the flesh, but to think that they had to become Jews in order to believe properly in Jesus Christ.

The second piece of advice, 5.16-17, gives a moral psychology; the human dilemma, which is perhaps a God-given check on man, is that he cannot do what he wants to do, because the flesh lusts against the spirit. The only remedy is to walk continually in the spirit and not pander to the flesh. I doubt if God's Holy Spirit is meant in this context, or that spirit and flesh are thought of as external powers or forces. "Spirit" and "flesh" in this context are probably the constituent parts of every man.

The section consists of three couplets. It is loosely related to the preceding section, of course, but on closer examination there is no inner connection between advice about how a man who is free should behave, and advice about how every man should understand the warfare going on within him.

The third saying, 5.18, is not an admonition at all, but a statement of moral fact. The Spirit is God's Spirit, in all probability, and this is a clear statement of Christian freedom. Those led by the Spirit are not under law because they do all that law requires and more. I do not think this is an antinomian statement, nor do I think it had any particular bearing on the problem facing the Galatians. They were tempted to become Jews not for moral reasons, but in order to be full children of Abraham and followers of Christ.

This verse is a couplet consisting of two short lines almost equal in length.

Verses 19-21 are a list of the works of the flesh that disqualify men from inheriting the Kingdom of God. The seemingly personal note in the beginning of the last triplet, "of this I warn you, as I warned you before", is not really personal, but simply a reminder that the Church must constantly listen to teachers who have always taught thus, and who continue to do so, in anticipation of the day of judgement, when the worthy will inherit God's Kingdom. Whether or not Paul would have spoken like this is a matter for debate, but I cannot see how this stylistically formal moral

68

admonition could have found a place in his urgent letter to the Galatians.

The piece consists of nine fairly even lines.

The fifth part, 5.22–3, might seem to belong with the fourth section, being a list of the fruits of the spirit in contrast to that of the works of the flesh. There is a relation—that is why they have been put together—but no real connection. This fifth part gives the fruits of the Holy Spirit which, when present in a man, guarantees that no law can be cited against him, whereas the fourth part listed the vices to be avoided by those who would inherit the Kingdom.

In form, too, these moral sayings are quite different. The fifth admonition is basically two sentences, the first sentence consisting of four cola, perhaps, in which the virtues are grouped in threes, but with nothing like the massive structure of the fourth admonition, with its nine stately lines. There is no direct correspondence between the vices in the first list and the virtues in the second.

The sixth part of the collection, 5.24, is the first one to mention Christ. It is a beautiful strophe, with four cola of almost equal length. The crucifixion is appropriated for the moral life of the Christian: to belong to Christ Jesus is to crucify the flesh in all its weakness and strength.

The seventh saying, 5.25, is an admonition to persevere in the spiritual life once begun. Although it consists of a couplet of two cola similar in length to the cola in verse 24, there is no connection either in style or in thought. The former is a statement and this is a conditional sentence; both are designed to make the reader see the consequences of what he claims for himself, but in different ways. The moral in each case is quite different, the former a call to self-denial, and the latter a call to perseverence.

The eighth saying, 5.26, is a straight command. It consists of three cola, the first forbidding the root tendency (conceit), the second condemning its positive manifestation (aggressiveness), and the third its negative manifestation (envy).

The ninth saying, 6.1, is a piece of advice in prose to the spiritual leaders of the Church about how they should deal with a moral offender. They should not be too harsh, and they should take care not to imperil their own moral character.

The tenth saying, 6.2, deals with relations between Christians. In contrast to the ninth saying, it does not particularly concern leaders of the community, and the burdens that have to be borne are not especially burdens caused by the moral failings of others. This is a prose saying. I doubt very much whether Paul could have employed such a phrase as "the law of Christ" in writing to the Galatians without a great deal of explanation; above all he emphasized to them that Christ had shown on the cross that no one could be justified by reliance on the Law, meaning by the Law the divine code that constituted Judaism. The phrase, "the law of Christ", transports us into an entirely different situation (despite 1 Cor. 9.21).

The eleventh saying, 6.3, is also in prose, but the form is conditional. This is a truism, of course, but it is meant to make the reader who does think he is someone ask himself whether he really is. Despite the γάρ, there is no connection between this statement, concerned with self-examination, and the preceding command to bear one another's burdens. The γάρ is probably simply a strengthening word like our "yes": "Yes, if anyone thinks he is something . . ." (cf. Didache 6.2, which has no inner connection with 6.1).

The twelfth moral statement, 6.4–5, is an exhortation to self-sufficiency in life. It is not logically compatible with 6.2, but one characteristic of proverbial wisdom is that incompatible sayings can live together quite happily, because they each get their point in rather different circumstances. This saying holds out to the moral pilgrim the hope of being able to say to himself that he owes his character to no one else; in any case, no one else can really shoulder his load.

The thirteenth piece of advice, 6.6, is probably an instruction to the student to share his whole wealth with his teacher. Perhaps it owes its place here to the fact that the previous word partly concerned the moral student who had to learn to stand on his own feet, but otherwise there is no connection between this verse and its context.

The fourteenth command, 6.7–8, has a poetic form again, the first in poetry since 5.26. It consists of four couplets, and warns the reader that he cannot escape the consequence of the decision he makes about the foundation of his life.

The final saying, 6.9–10, is a prose command, linked with the preceding one because of the catch-word "reap", but not really connected. The point of this advice is that Christians should persevere in doing good, especially in doing good to fellow-Christians. The fourteenth saying was individual, but the fifteenth social;

although both look ahead to the ultimate consequence of our actions now, the former concerns the basic choice to be made, and the latter the behaviour to be followed day after day.

The whole collection of sayings is Christian, although it incorporates pieces of wisdom drawn from Jewish and Greek sources. There is no inner idea running through the collection, although each saying shares the family likeness. Weisse and Cramer both attempted to eliminate certain sayings as non-Pauline, but Völter was nearer the truth when he suggested that 5.13–6.11 was a later addition to Galatians. I can find nothing specifically Pauline in the collection, and nothing that would have had specific bearing on the situation facing the Galatians. The collection was probably added to the epistle at an appropriate place because an epistle meant for building up the Church at large would need to have its own ethical section. The man who added this section did not, of course, make up any of the teaching himself, but merely inserted the corpus traditional in his church; he may well have thought that it derived from Paul.

1. *Gesetz und Geist: Eine Untersuchung zur Vorgeschichte des Galaterbriefes* (Gütersloh 1919).
2. *The Singular Problem of the Epistle to the Galatians* (Cambridge, Mass., 1929): "... this passage [5.13ff] calls imperatively for the explanation which Lütgert's theory supplies" (p. 40).
3. See W. G. Kümmel, *Einleitung in das Neue Testament* (13th edn of Feine-Behm, Heidelberg 1964), pp. 193f; English translation of the 14th edn (1966), pp. 194f.
4. "Die Häretiker in Galatien", *ZNW* 47 (1956), pp. 25–67.
5. See particularly section 5 of his essay, ibid., pp. 50–5.

6.16   omit και επι τον Ισραηλ του θεου

Paul seems to have reserved the word "Israel" for the Jewish nation. In the present context, he can hardly have meant to bless the whole of Israel (Cramer), irrespective of whether or not they held to the canon of the cross of Christ; Rom. 9.1–5; 10.1; 11.1, to which Cramer refers, are hardly relevant at this point in Paul's present argument. Nor can he be referring to the Jewish Christians (Rückert, Hofmann), nor to "those within Israel to whom God will show mercy" (P. Richardson, *Israel in the Apostolic Church* (1969), p. 82; cf. Burton). On that showing, the emphatic ὅσοι at the beginning of the verse would be weakened, if not completely contradicted. Either these Jews would be included among those who would walk according to the rule to which Paul is appealing, in which case they need not be specifically mentioned, or they would not be going to follow this rule, in which case their mention would require a much fuller justification than this bare mention affords.

The only conclusion to be drawn is that the words "even upon the Israel of God" refer to the Church, and that they are commentary on the words "all who will walk according to this rule". Paul himself, however, could not possibly have departed so casually from his normal usage. He held that "not all Israel is Israel" (Rom. 9.6), and he also held that Gentiles as well as Jews could be sons of Abraham (Gal. 3.7, 29; 4.31; Rom. 4.10–12), but he never used "Israel" to refer to the one Church, made up of Jews and Gentiles.

The phrase "Israel of God" is a tell-tale sign that the words printed at the head of this note are a gloss. The implication is that there is a false Israel as well as a true Israel, and that they are two organized entities. Paul believed that the descendants of Israel had to choose whether or not to be true to Abraham (cf. 4.28—5.1), but he does not distinguish two Israels. (If 1 Cor. 10.18 is an exception, it can scarcely belong to Paul.) Nor does he apply the term "Israel" to all who believe in Jesus Christ, for his special apostolic work is to bring Gentiles as Gentiles to inherit the promise made for them to Abraham. Believing Gentiles become Abraham's sons, but not part of Israel.

The gloss was added at a time when the Church and Israel were sharply distinguished, when Jews who believed could no longer remain within Israel because they could not recite the Test Benediction. Perhaps, indeed, the gloss is a deliberate appropriation of another of the Benedictions, the nineteenth, which runs, in the Babylonian recension, "Give peace, happiness, and blessing, grace, lovingkindness, and mercy upon us and upon all Israel your people . . . " The gloss reflects an age when the Church, made up of Gentiles and Jews, saw itself as the true Israel, and this was an age much later than Paul's.

A SUMMARY OF THE EPISTLE

The analysis of the Epistle to the Galatians which I have worked out is necessarily tentative and hypothetical. Nevertheless, the attempt should be made to generalize and make explicit the results of the analysis. The consistency of the picture of Paul's theology that emerges will be one test of the likelihood of the thesis. A generalization of the results may also help in an analysis of the other Pauline epistles, although it is important that the analysis of each epistle should begin with the inconsistencies and uneven transitions in the text itself, rather than start from a general picture to which Paul must be made to conform.

Paul did not emerge as a thinker whose ideas could be described by one or two labels; if he had, I should have begun to doubt the validity of this approach, fearing that my analysis was an unconscious attempt to escape from the complexity of a flesh-and-blood man by imagining a more manageable abstraction. But Paul's thought, in the portions of the Epistle to the Galatians that I conjecture came from him, is both rich and complex.

The following brief summary is an attempt to gather up the results of my previous discussions, and to show that the epistle which I conjecture Paul wrote is reasonably clear and consistent. I have added a note in brackets after the summarizing paragraphs to indicate what major changes in Paul's argument the glossators, wittingly or unwittingly, had brought about.

Paul writes as an apostle commissioned not by man, but directly by Jesus Christ and God the Father who raised him from the dead. Paul is not an isolated apostle; he is surrounded by fellow-workers, who agree with his appeal to the Galatian churches. The apostolic blessing contains a reminder of the preaching of the cross; by Jesus Christ's giving himself for our sins, we are delivered from the present age by the will of God our Father. (1.1–5)

Paul is amazed that the Galatian churches have so quickly turned away to follow another piece of good news—which isn't really good news. His amazement is tempered by discovering that the speed of the defection is due to trouble-makers who are perverting the good news of Christ. Whoever comes to them—Paul himself or even an angel—with good news different from the first good news, let him be cursed. (1.6–9)

(Paul's polemic is sharp, and he is fighting for what he believes to be certain truth, but the dispute is still within the bounds of the Christian faith. The glossator in 1.6 thought otherwise, and assumed that the Galatians had already defected from God. By removing the gloss we recover a possible historical setting for the epistle.)

Paul argues that it would be unthinkable for him now to try to curry favour with the Galatians by changing his mind. To please men would be to stop being a servant of Christ. His good news is not tailored to men's preconceptions. He did not get it from men and was not taught it. He received it by Jesus Christ's revealing himself to him. (1.10–12)

God had marked him out before he was born, and graciously called him to be an apostle. When it pleased God, God revealed his Son to him in order that he should carry the good news of the Son to the Gentiles. As soon as this revelation occurred, Paul did not consult with men, and did not go to Jerusalem to the apostles who were apostles before him, but went to Arabia. He then returned to Damascus. (1.15–17)

Three years later he went to Jerusalem to get information from Cephas about the Lord's words and deeds before the resurrection. He stayed two weeks, and saw no other apostle except James, the Lord's brother. He swears to that. Then he went to Syria and Cilicia. (1.18–21)

(The removal of 1.13, 14, 22–4 cuts away biographical material that obscures Paul's case. Paul himself would scarcely have turned aside from an argument designed to show his independence as an apostle to remind the Galatians of what they knew already, that he was once an exemplary Jew who persecuted the Church and who was the hero of a ballad sung in the provincial congregations of Judea. Nor is Paul himself likely to have spoken so distantly of Judaism, as though it were another religion altogether.)

Fourteen years after his previous visit Paul took Titus and went with Barnabas to Jerusalem again. His journey was in obedience to a command from God. In private session with the leaders of the Jerusalem church he laid before them the gospel he preached to the Gentiles. He wanted a private meeting, in case the work proved to be in vain because the Jerusalem leaders were not yet ready to receive this gathering in of the Gentiles. (2.1–2)

(The excision of one word in 2.2 removes any suggestion of two meetings, a public one as well as a private one. Paul and Barnabas consulted the "pillars" in private, and therefore the public discussion in Acts 15 is not likely to refer to Paul's second visit to Jerusalem after his conversion.)

However, not even his companion, who was a Greek, was compelled to be circumcised because of the pressure exerted by the false brothers. These had been coming in to Paul's Gentile congregations and threatening the freedom they had in Christ Jesus and attempting to enslave them. Paul and his fellow-workers had never for a moment yielded to these men, who made themselves out to be important. Paul doesn't care what grand positions they once held. God does not pay any attention to that sort of thing. (2.3–6a)

(The usual text of Galatians here is difficult and obscure, so difficult and obscure that some commentators have concluded that Titus was in fact circumcised.[1] The obscurity arose, I believe, because someone thought that the case of Timothy's circumcision was relevant, and should be allowed for. The gloss had one further unfortunate effect, in suggesting that Paul somehow identified the self-appointed worthies, whom he execrates, with the Jerusalem pillars, whom he honours.)

The authorities in Jerusalem did not lay any requirements on Paul, accepting his work whole-heartedly and recognizing that God had given him the task of carrying the good news to the Gentiles. Just as God was at work in the mission to Jews, so he was at work in Paul's mission to Gentiles. James, Cephas, and John, the pillars of Israel, recognized God's grace in Paul's work and gave Paul and Barnabas the right hand of fellowship, in recognition that they should go primarily to Jews and Paul and Barnabas to Gentiles. The only condition was that Paul and Barnabas should remember the poor of Jerusalem, and Paul was eager to do that. (2.6b–10)

(This section has been left untouched by glossators, except for the one who imported two references to Peter's primacy in the Jewish congregations.)

When Cephas came to Antioch, Paul withstood him because he was clearly in the wrong. Before he left James he had eaten with Gentiles, but on arriving in Antioch he stopped that practice and withdrew, because he was afraid of the Jews. The rest of the Jewish Christians followed his example, and even Barnabas was carried away by their hypocritical behaviour. (2.11–13)

(One small addition and a consequent change of one letter have been sufficient to make James into a sinister figure in the history of the early Church. What I think Paul actually wrote must now, on the contrary, be put to James's credit. James may well have been the man who was able to keep Cephas firm against Jewish pressure so long as the two men were together. Only when Cephas left James did he give in to his compatriots and cease to eat with Gentiles.)

When Paul saw that the Jewish Christians in Antioch had ceased to act according to the truth of the good news, he publicly confronted Peter with the following argument. If Peter as a Jew continued to observe Jewish customs, how could he put pressure on Gentiles to stop being Gentiles and become Jews? Both he and Peter were Jews by nature and not sinners in the way Gentiles were. Yet they both also knew that a man was not justified by keeping the Law, unless he had faith in Christ Jesus. They had both put their faith in Christ in order to be justified by faith in him and not by doing the works of the Law. As Scripture said, No flesh is justified, meaning, by the works of the Law. (2.14–16)

(The omission of three words in 2.14 restores Paul's argument against Cephas to the realm of historical probability. The uncorrected text makes Paul into an impossibly feeble debater. First, he seems to assume an interpretation of Cephas's conduct that neither Cephas nor his contemporaries would regard as at all self-evident. Second, he accuses Cephas of inconsistency at just the moment when Cephas has abandoned what could have been regarded as inconsistency. Paul seems to be both condemning the change of policy and wanting Cephas to remain inconsistent so that he could be attacked on logical grounds. When we see that the three words are a gloss, Paul's argument becomes perfectly clear, and the sequel follows. Verse 17 goes out on the same grounds, that it completely obscures the surrounding argument on any of the attempts to work it in. By itself the verse makes good sense as a general theological reflection, unrelated to the Galatian situation.)

Paul argued that if he (or, by implication, Cephas) started to re-erect barriers that he had begun to break down in obedience to

76

God, he would show himself a transgressor. His whole life was, by definition, a life of faith in God who loved him and gave himself for him. He could not now reject the gift of God, which was the free forgiveness of sinners who had broken his Law. If it were possible to keep the Law, Christ would not have needed to die. Christians have taken the full weight of the Law and recognized that they are sinners. Since they are sinners, the Law can no longer help them, and their only hope is to accept crucifixion with Christ and so put their whole trust in God's forgiving love. (2.18–21)

(The first sentence of verse 20 gives a mystical interpretation to Paul's words. Paul had used the metaphor of death to denote a radical change of aim and expectation. The glossator uses the metaphor to denote a radical change of nature or being. Paul said, "I once lived under the Law, expecting to be able to please God by keeping the Law, but I have now learnt through Christ's death that I can only live by faith in God's grace." The glossator interpreted this change in living as a change in actual substance: "I no longer live, but Christ lives in me".)

Paul turns to the Galatians and addresses them directly. How can they have been so foolish; who can have so totally bewitched them, as to deny the vision of Christ crucified? He demands an answer to the question whether they received the Spirit by doing the works of the Law or by faith, whether God gave the Spirit and wonderful signs so lavishly to them when they did the works, or when they had faith. (3.1–5)

(A glossator took πίστις in 3.2 and 5 to mean the Christian Faith, and surmised that, as the Law required works, so The Christian Faith required hearing. Paul originally meant that faith, meaning belief and trust, was the true way to approach God, in contrast to the impossible way of works. Verses 3 and 4 are also glosses, which moralize about beginning spiritually and ending carnally, and so obscure Paul's argument that the present possession of the Spirit by the Galatians is proof that they do not have to accept circumcision in order to be full Christians.)

They know that men who have faith are sons of Abraham. Scripture knew beforehand that God would justify Gentiles by faith, and records the good news that all the Gentiles were to be blessed in him. So those who have faith are blessed with Abraham, the man of faith. (3.7–9)

77

(An apposite, but unnecessary, proof text has been copied into the text from the margin (verse 6).)

Those who tried to live by keeping all the commandments of the Law were under a curse, as Scripture says when it states that any man who fails to keep everything written in the Law is cursed. It is obvious that no one is justified before God by the Law because "the righteous man shall live by faith", and the Law is not of faith because "the man who *does* these things shall live in them". Christ redeemed us from the curse of the Law by becoming for us a curse in being crucified. This was in order that the Gentiles might at last receive the blessing of Abraham, so that all might receive the promised Spirit. (3.10–14)

Paul adduces an argument that holds on the analogy of similar human affairs. Promises were made to Abraham and his descendants. The fact that God many years later gave the Law cannot nullify the earlier covenant into which he had entered; he cannot have meant to withdraw the promise made earlier. If the unconditional promise were later made to depend on a legal condition, it would no longer be a pure promise. God was graciously pleased to deal with Abraham by making a pure promise. (3.15–18)

(In 3.15 a glossator has worked on the assumption that the Law was an illegitimate attempt, by "God" other than the God who made the original covenant with Abraham, to change the original provisions. This conflicts with Paul's assumption that God who made the covenant with Abraham also gave the Law to Moses, although the glossator was given some grounds for making his point by Paul's argument that the giving of the Law was not meant to change the basic relation between God and his people established with the promise to Abraham. The gloss in 3.16, which depends on an unreal verbal point about "seed" not being "seeds", is well recognized by commentators.)

What then was the point of the Law? It was introduced in order to check transgressions, until the descendants of Abraham to whom the promise was made should arise. The Law is not the enemy of the promises; it is simply not strong enough to bring to life men who will be righteous. If it had been strong enough, then righteousness would have been based on keeping the Law. But Scripture makes perfectly plain that all men are under sin, so that the promise based on faith can be given only to those who have faith. (3.19–22)

(In 3.19, 20 a glossator has again exaggerated the extent to which Paul wished to give the Law the second place to the promise. He suggested that the employment of Moses as mediator implied that the Law originated with the heavenly host rather than with God himself. Verses 23–5 are another long gloss, written to cast light on the general moral problem concerning the place of moral discipline and restraint in the growth of the human personality. This argument, important as it is, has nothing to do with the Galatians, who are facing a specific campaign to make them adopt the whole Law of Moses.)

Paul concludes that the Galatians are sons of Abraham through having faith. By baptism they were enrolled as the Messiah's people; if they are the Messiah's they are naturally also Abraham's, and heirs in accordance with the promise made to Abraham long ago. (3.26–9)

(A glossator has added 3.28, a striking affirmation of the unity of all the baptized, but an affirmation which Paul could hardly have made without a great deal more explanation than is given here.)

Because the Galatians are Christ's they are Abraham's, and because they are Abraham's sons, God has given them his Spirit so that they call him Father. Each of them is no longer servant but son, and each son is therefore heir of the original promise to Abraham.

The argument began and ended with the plain fact that the Galatians had received the Spirit by faith without becoming Jews. They were full sons of Abraham already, and could not be required to become Jewish proselytes. (4.6–7)

(Perhaps not surprisingly, this section of Paul's argument has been heavily glossed. The first gloss, in all probability, was a Jewish Christian hymn concerning the incarnation by the Blessed Virgin Mary (4.4–5). It is not surprising that this ancient hymn was inserted here, because it recognized the Law as in some sense a slave master from which the incarnate Son would free his own in order that they should by adoption become sons.

The other major gloss consists of 4.1–3, 8–10. This assumes, in contrast to Paul and the author of the Jewish Christian hymn, that men are naturally sons and heirs, but that they are oppressed by cosmic powers, from which they needed to be delivered. The deliverance has come about by the gnosis they have received. The author of this comment is now pleading with Christians not to go back into the cosmic bondage, from which they have already been delivered, by giving themselves up again to the observance of elaborate calendric festivals in order to placate the astral forces.)

The next section of Paul's argument is a personal appeal to the loyalty of the Galatians. It contains some expressions obscure to us, but no doubt clear enough to them.

In general Paul reminds the Galatians that they did not at all despise him, though despise him they might, when he first came to them a sick man. They would have given him their own eyes, if they could, to repair his wretched sight. Is he now their enemy because he is bold enough to tell them the truth about their stupidity in listening to other advice? He wishes they would be as devoted to him when he is absent as they were when he was present. He is as concerned about them now as he was in the early days of his mission to them; he wishes he could come himself and speak differently from the tone in which he is forced to write. (4.11–20)

(In 4.17 we seem to have a comment that reflects a later claim by the Jewish Christian churches to excommunicate Gentile Christian congregations that would not conform. Verse 19 contains a striking spiritual metaphor which compares the work of an evangelist with the conception of Christ in the womb of his people, the people being likened to the Virgin Mary.)

Paul throws down a challenge to those who have swallowed the propaganda and wish to live under the Law. What do they make of the accounts in the Law itself?

Abraham had two sons, Ishmael son of a slave woman, and Isaac born of a free woman. The first was born in the natural course of events, but the second as the result of a promise. This distinction has allegorical meaning. You Galatians may see yourselves there in Isaac, for you, like him, are children as a result of the promise. Just as the naturally conceived son persecuted the spiritually conceived son, so unbelieving Jews persecute the heirs of the promise. Persecution is a sign that they are children of the free woman rather than children of the slave. (4.21–31)

(The famous allegory of the two mothers, Sarah and Hagar, representing the heavenly Jerusalem and the earthly Jerusalem, comes from a time much later in the history of the Church than Paul's. The allegory assumes that Judaism and Christianity are two separate entities. Paul, however, is working on the assumption that the Jewish Christians, under the leadership of the "pillars" in Jerusalem, and accepting gladly the existence of separate Gentile Christian churches who showed their loyalty and gratitude by sending money to Jerusalem, were the true nucleus of Israel, to which the unbelieving Jews might yet turn. Consequently, I hold that 4.24b–27, 30 are later comments. If it is not possible to isolate 4.21–24a, 28, 29, 31 as Paul's, then the whole of 4.21–31 must be a later comment.)

Christ has freed them to remain free. They must on no account take on the yoke of slavery. Paul has to warn them solemnly that Christ will be of no benefit to them if they accept circumcision. Anyone who accepted circumcision would be obliged to keep the whole Law; those who thought to attain righteousness by keeping the Law would cut themselves off from Christ and would forfeit his gift. (5.1–4)

The position is this. Christians had the Spirit, and so lived in expectation of becoming righteous on the basis of trust. In Christ it did not matter whether you were a Jew or a Gentile; what mattered was a man's trust in God, worked out through love. (5.5–6)

They had been running well. Paul asks who it was who had put obstacles in the way of their obeying the truth. He certainly, who had first called them to obedience, was not responsible for this persuasion. A little leaven was capable of leavening the whole lump, and one trouble-maker could disaffect the whole body of believers. He was persuaded, as he trusted the Lord, that they did not really want to adhere to this quite other teaching. The trouble-maker, whoever he was, would have to face the consequences of what he was doing when he came before the judgement seat. If Paul was preaching circumcision (as perhaps the trouble-maker had suggested), why should he continue to be persecuted? If he did proclaim circumcision, he would destroy the cross as the stumbling-block to human pretensions, the stumbling-block which brought forgiveness to those who would admit they were sinners. He wishes those men who were upsetting the Galatians would turn their knives on themselves. Then they would understand what they were trying to do to the Galatians by preaching circumcision. (5.7–12)

(A glossator thought that Paul's circumcising of Timothy implied that he had once preached circumcision, and inserted the first "still" in 5.11. The charge that Paul did preach circumcision may well have arisen over the Timothy incident, but Paul could not possibly have admitted that he had ever done what he was accused of, nor would he have been right to do so, on our evidence.)

(No apostolic letter could be allowed to go out without its portion of positive advice about the Christian life. A commentator has accordingly inserted at a convenient point before Paul's peroration an old collection of moral aphorisms, 5.13—6.10. These aphorisms have nothing in particular to do with the urgent choices facing the Galatians, but they help to make the epistle more generally useful for preaching and instruction in the universal Church.)

In 6.11 Paul notes that he himself has taken the pen from the amanuensis; they can tell by observing the large letters which a man of poor sight has to make.

Those who compel the Galatians to be circumcised are wanting to make the Christians more acceptable to men by getting them to conform to religious observances that might escape persecution. But they are bound to be persecuted for the cross of Christ; the cross itself was the end result of persecution, and those who adhere to it will also be persecuted. (6.11–12)

Those men who are circumcised do not themselves keep the Law, but they want the Galatians to be circumcised in order to boast to their fellow-Jews that a crucified Messiah does not imply that his followers ignore the Law. Paul boasts only in the sacrifice made by Jesus Christ on the cross. By that cross he no longer cares for the approval of men for his own heroism, and no longer seeks to win that approval. The fact that he is a Jew and the Galatians are Gentiles is nothing; all that matters is the new creation, in which the fall of Adam is to be reversed.

(A later glossator would distinguish between Judaism, the faithless Israel, and Christianity, the true Israel, but Paul thought rather of Israel and the Gentiles. "Israel" for him meant all Jews or all Jews who believed, but not the one Church made up of Gentiles and Jews. The mission of the "pillars" at Jerusalem was to bring back the circumcision, as Paul's mission was to bring in the Gentiles. The glossator sharply distinguished "God's Israel" from the earthly apostate Judaism.)

Paul is about to be martyred; he is about to bear the marks of Jesus on his body. (This is the interpretation of Karl Schrader, followed by R. Steck.) He hopes, therefore, that he will not be troubled by news that the Galatians are going any further along the dangerous path they have been tempted to follow. He closes with a blessing, that the gift of the Lord Jesus Christ might remain with them. (6.17–18)

NOTE

1. F. C. Burkitt, *Christian Beginnings: Three Lectures* (1924), p. 118: ". . . for who can doubt that it was the knife which really did circumcise Titus that has cut the syntax of Gal. ii 3–5 to pieces?" Burkitt is followed by Duncan.

CONCLUSION

Throughout this book I have often attempted to solve exegetical puzzles by arguing that they have come about because comments by later writers have been incorporated into the original text. The method suffers from a great danger. The exegete is tempted to wield the scalpel before he has exhausted less drastic means of understanding the apparent disease. I am inclined to think the patient's condition is more serious than has been supposed. Each case must in the end be decided on its own merits, yet nevertheless there is room for a general vindication of the method. In the following paragraphs I shall try to show that the general types of corruption I detect are not improbable, and that the procedure I follow is not arbitrary.

Many of the additions to which I have drawn attention are already omitted by some manuscripts of Galatians, and there is no objection in principle to accepting the shorter text in these cases.

Some of the shorter omissions for which I have argued, however, are not supported by direct textual evidence; and indeed sometimes they are not supported by the presence of any textual disturbance at all in the surrounding context. There have always been textual critics who have made conjectural changes in the received texts without manuscript evidence, and many of these conjectures, made by such men as Beza, Richard Bentley, Paul Schmiedel, and a host of others, are still discussed in the commentaries.[1] This approach has very much fallen out of favour, and most critics today regard the vast amount of manuscript evidence as reducing the probability that a reading entirely unsupported should be original.

I see the force of this objection when the conjecture is that one word has been misread for another; it does not seem likely that *no* manuscript should preserve a word which, to the modern critic, seems to make better sense. However, that is not the only type of conjecture.

My reason for being more hopeful about conjecture is based on the hypothesis that the commonest contamination of a text so well transmitted as the text of the New Testament does not stem from mistaking a word, but rather from repeated attempts to make the text clearer by added explanation. I should like to propose the axiom that the commonest form of corruption of a sacred text is the addition of a gloss.

In that case I believe we are justified in reversing the usual strictures against conjecture.

I propose a further axiom for the critic who is prepared to abandon the ruling orthodoxy and set out once more on the quest of the earliest text by means of conjecture. The principle would run like this. The existence of a number of various readings in one sentence or paragraph raises the probability that the text is corrupt; but it is quite possible that no one manuscript preserves the earliest text, and the conjectured text most likely to be correct is the one that explains the highest proportion of variants.

If that is so, are there any principles for deciding whether or not any words are glosses once added to the original text? The basic principle to note is that only the unsuccessful gloss will be detectable. An unsuccessful gloss is either (i) a gloss that tries to meet a difficulty that is unreal. It may be unreal because the glossator has not understood the sense of the original, or has understood it in the light of conditions in his own day that did not apply in the day of the author. Or an unsuccessful gloss is (ii) a gloss that was quite correct as a gloss, but which causes difficulties when it is incorporated into the original text.

The tests to be applied to words that are suspected of being a gloss are (a) that they explain a plausible difficulty which lies in the text minus the words in question, and (b) that the removal of the words leaves a text which is free from stubborn difficulties that have long perplexed scholars, but yet contains the sort of difficulty to invite the attention of a glossator.

These are the rules, if they can rightly be called rules, upon which I have proceeded.

Even if the reader is prepared to allow for the possibility of the short glosses I have been describing, he may well draw back from the further possibility that is assumed in these pages. This is the possibility that longer passages of commentary have also been added to the original epistle. It is not too hard to imagine that words and phrases written in the margins of copies of the epistle were later copied into the text, but it seems much harder to understand how longer passages, such as Galatians 1.13–14, 22–

24; part of 2.20; 3.23–5; 3.28; 4.1–3, 8–10; 4.24b–27; or 5.13—6.10, could possibly have been incorporated into our epistle.

The shorter comments of this nature could have come in in the same way as the glosses consisting of a few words. A remark in the margin could have been incorporated by a later scribe, under the impression that the marginal words represented the correction of an omission. But the longer passages are harder to explain on this supposition.

The only explanation must be that Paul's epistle was edited for publication some time after it had been in use for preaching and teaching. At that stage the editor felt free to add material, perhaps on the grounds that its antiquity guaranteed its authenticity. That was surely the reason why the moral admonitions in 5.13—6.10 came to be incorporated into the epistle. If Paul's epistle was used in preaching and teaching, an editor could understandably assume that well-established interpretative comments had a right to a place in the final text.

This is not simply my own supposition. There are examples of other sacred texts in the early history of the Church which were edited according to these rules, as far as we can see. The seven Epistles of Ignatius that are commonly regarded as original today were always supplemented by further pseudonymous epistles, and often themselves corrupted by interpolations, in the manuscripts we possess. These interpolations, which we can detect because we also possess manuscripts containing shorter versions of the genuine epistles, were made in the same way as the longer interpolations I am supposing were added to Galatians.

There are great risks attached to the kind of criticism I have employed. The only justification is that the present text of Galatians contains such obscurity, inconsequence, and contradiction that some solution must be found. If the choice lies between supposing that Paul was confused and contradictory and supposing that his text has been commented upon and enlarged, I have no hesitation in choosing the second. Justice to Paul carries with it the incidental advantage of doing justice to the good and earnest men who first tried to make Paul plain to their contemporaries.

The aim is to hear Paul, for he is *an apostle, not from men, but through Jesus Christ, and through God the Father who raised Jesus Christ from the dead.*

NOTE

1. The most famous collection of conjectures is the list published at the end of William Bowyer's two-volume New Testament (1763) reprinted separately as *Critical Conjectures and Observations on the New Testament, Collected from Various Authors, As well in regard to Words as Pointing: With the Reasons on Which Both are Founded* (1772; 3rd edn, 1782; 4th edn, 1812). See B. M. Metzger, *The Text of the New Testament: Its Transmission, Corruption and Restoration* (2nd edn, 1968), pp. 115–16, 182–5.